FROM MOHAIR
SUITS TO
KINKY BOOTS

FROM MOHAIR SUITS TO KINKY BOOTS

Geoff Deane

**MUSWELL
PRESS**

First published by Muswell Press in 2023
Copyright © Geoff Deane 2023

Introduction copyright © Maurice Gran 2023

Typeset in Bembo by M Rules

Printed and bound by
CPI Group (UK) Ltd, Croydon CR0 4YY

A CIP catalogue record for this book
is available from the British Library

ISBN: 9781739471637
eISBN: 9781739193003

Muswell Press
London N6 5HQ
www.muswell-press.co.uk

For the saucepan lids, Woody, Nelly and Otis.
And my friends, Jacky and Bruno.

*'Outside of a dog, a book is man's best friend.
Inside of a dog it's too dark to read.'*

Groucho Marx

Contents

Glossary

86: to throw out

Adam and Eve: believe

Aris: from bottle and glass, arse. Shortened to bottle, rhyming with Aristotle, then shortened again to Aris

Barnet: from Barnet Fair – hair

Boat: from boat race – face

Brassic/boracic: from boracic lint – skint

Bristol: from Bristol City – titty/breast

Brown bread: dead

Bugle: nose

Bunny: from rabbit and pork – talk

Buntz: profit (Yiddish)

Claret: blood

Clobber: clothes

Cream crackered: knackered, tired

Crew: gang

Deuce and ace: face

Dog and bone: phone

Drum: abode, home

Farmer Giles: piles

Four-by-two: Jew

Full SP: from bookies' starting prices – the whole situation

Gaff: building or premises

Gander: from Gander's hook – look

Gary Glitter: shitter/toilet

Gooner: Gunner, Arsenal fan

Gornisht: nothing (Yiddish)

Gregory Peck: cheque, or neck

Half-inch: to pinch, steal

Hampsteads: from Hampstead Heath – teeth

Hampton: from Hampton Wick – prick

Handle: name

Hobson's choice: voice

Hooky: dodgy, crooked

Irish goodbye: leaving a gathering without telling anyone

Jack and Danny: fanny

Jacksy: backside/bottom

Jim and Jack: back

Kenny Market: Kensington Market

Knocked off: stolen

Lallies: legs (Polari)

Larry Large/giving it Larry: giving it the big one.
    acting leary

Melt: someone soft, pathetic

Mince pie: eye

Moniker: name

Moody: false, fake

Nisht: nothing (Yiddish)

Old Bill: police

Pie-and-mash point: cash point

Povvo: poor

Radio rental: mental, crazy

Riddims: rhythm (Patois)

Rosy Lea: tea

Schlep: drag, carry (Yiddish)

Schmear: the spread on a beigel/bagel. Usually cream cheese (Yiddish)

Schmooze: sweet talk (Yiddish)

Schmuck: idiot (Yiddish)

Schmutter: clothes or fabric (Yiddish)

Schneid: fake (Yiddish)

Score, A: £20

Scotch pegs: legs

Septic tank: Yank

Sexton Blake: steak

Shades: sunglasses

Shechita: kosher slaughterhouse (Yiddish)

Sheitel: wig worn by Orthodox Jewish woman (Yiddish)

Sherbet: alcoholic drink

Skyrocket: pocket

Sort: attractive girl or woman

Spieler: gambler (Yiddish)

Spondulix: Cash

Squid: quid, i.e. £1.00

Strides: trousers

Syrup: from syrup of figs – wig

Tchotchke: small decorative object (Yiddish)

Titfer: from tit for tat – hat

Ton: hundred

Two and eight: a state

Wallah: a person concerned with a specified thing or business

Whistle: from whistle and flute – suit

Autobiographies are for people who have led truly extraordinary lives. Or those so famous you don't notice they haven't led truly extraordinary lives. I'm neither. So what we have here is a collection of musings and recollections that I hope will entertain. If anything you read should move you or provoke serious thought I am humbled. But all I really care about is the laughs.

GEOFF DEANE

INTRODUCTION

I am a mild and lazy guy, the kind of writer who likes making things up in the warmth of his spare room, rather than having experiences and writing about them. I suspect Geoff Deane is the opposite. He probably didn't set out to be any kind of writer, but merely to have a hell of a life. I bet that from the moment his voice broke – probably at the age of nine – his plan was to have as much fun as possible every single day, to sing, dance, drink, smoke, snort, screw, laugh, love and repeat.

When I met Geoff, around 1990, he was knee-deep in life and loving every minute of it. He had already enjoyed one career as a singer with East London pop-punksters the Leyton Buzzards, and another salsa-ing around the globe with his next band, Modern Romance. They always seemed to be on Top of the Pops in the early eighties, having more fun than anyone in the studio with the possible exception of Jimmy Saville. When the band split up, Geoff became obsessed with situation comedy. Obsessions tend to come thick and fast with Mr Deane. He segued into comedy writing and joined the team on *Birds of a Feather*, the hit sitcom I co-created, about two Essex girls whose husbands had been sent to prison. Geoff took to the show like a duck to another, really cute,

1

duck. He understood these characters: he'd grown up around them in the East End, he knew how they spoke, he knew how they thought, and he was funny with it.

After a couple of very successful years on *Birds*, Geoff buggered off and set up his own production company – in competition with mine, the cheeky sod – and started churning out sitcoms and movies. I moved out of London to the Cotswolds, while he went from the suburbs back into the East End, the week before Shoreditch supplanted Notting Hill; his timing was always impeccable. Our paths didn't cross so often but now and again I'd run into him holding court at the Groucho or some cooler dive. He was always good company, and always seemed to be working on something exciting and glamorous. He told me about a film he was writing about a Drag Queen's quest for the perfect shoe. That'll never work I recall thinking. But I would allow myself the occasional twinge of envy. He was off to Hollywood. I was stuck in Borehamwood.

Then Covid came and all Geoff's favourite clubs, pubs, dives and dens were closed down. What was he to do with himself? And suddenly, at least it seemed sudden to me, perfect little essays started to appear in Geoff's Facebook feed (is that the right term? I'm quite old). Tales of first love and lust, dodgy jobs, nights out, punch-ups won, lost or narrowly avoided, and of how he and his bandmates conquered the Post Punk/New Romantic/Glamrock/Rude Boy pop scenes through force of character, and monumental quantities of *chutzpah*. Stories tall, short and wide. Stories I started to look out for, because to say Geoff has a way with words is to use a pallid cliché in praise of a true stylist. Geoff knows what he wants to say, and he knows how to say it. He'd had more adventures than seemed remotely possible, and now he was sharing them with us, his grateful locked-down followers.

If I had been braver, ballsier, taller, I could have grown up to be Geoff Deane. Instead, I was just one of many who enjoyed his irregular bulletins and urged, begged and pleaded with him to expand them into a book. Finally Geoff succumbed to our flattery. I was thrilled until he asked me if I would write an introduction. Obviously I had to say yes: after all, he wouldn't have written the damn thing if I hadn't nagged him.

I happened to be on the train to Liverpool when I opened my laptop and began working my way through a file of Geoff's stories. Very quickly I was unable to prevent snorts, chuckles and guffaws from forcing their way out of nose and mouth. Soon I was helpless, laughing out loud. Not many books can do that. One or two fellow passengers gave me the sort of glare that says, 'This is supposed to be the quiet carriage and if I wasn't English, I'd call the guard.'

I couldn't help it. Geoff's lust for life and his eye for detail combine repeatedly to deadly effect. He has adventures where other people don't even have experiences, and the folks he meets – some 'normal', others extraordinary, he renders effortlessly into the sort of characters you'd be delighted to encounter in a damn good road movie.

At this stage in the proceedings I think I'm expected to extract from the text, for your edification and entertainment, a bouquet of bons mots, a clutch of witticisms, a jar of jokes and a gaggle of gags. But you've got the bloody book in your hands, read it already!

MAURICE GRAN, June 2023

STRAIGHT OUTTA HACKNEY

In late 1969 we moved away from the council flats in Amhurst Road, Hackney. A place I loved and the only home I had ever known. My dad had got a better job, which allowed my parents to take out their first mortgage. The new flat in leafy North Chingford had cost the princely sum of £5,400. I can still recall the family's trepidation at taking on such a fearful financial responsibility.

In truth, it was a good time to move. Most of the people we knew were being rehoused in newly built tower blocks. Ominous-looking monoliths that cast their brutalist shadow over the neighbourhood. This simple switch from living horizontally to vertically would kill a community's life force at the stroke of some authority planner's biro. Mums who had once stood out on balconies having a natter with 'her next door' while they kept an eye on the kids playing below would now not see their neighbours from one month to the next.

When they did, it was usually in a lift that stank of piss.

But hey, the flats had central heating. Yay.

So I was pleased to swerve them but broken-hearted about

leaving the flats. Living there would always remain amongst my happiest memories. There was so much I would miss about them, not least my family, most of whom seemed to reside there.

Beneath us was my Uncle Sid and his four boys. Known locally as 'Joe Cunt', Sid was a taxi driver and streetfighter who also minded the door at the notorious Regency Club, just down the road. Being a somewhat chippy geezer, my uncle always thought people were taking liberties with him. On such occasions he was often heard to utter the phrase, 'Do I look like my name's Joe Cunt?' At some point everyone in the community decided the answer to that was a resounding 'yes', and the nickname stuck. Even his missus, my Auntie Milly, called him Joe Cunt.

Opposite us was my Auntie Bessy, who weighed in at a healthy thirty-four stone. She was apparently a good-looking woman in her day, though no one could tell me exactly when that day was. Her husband was a bald little bloke named Will whom she always affectionately referred to as 'shithouse'. The only thing these two had in common was that his weight went into hers exactly four times. A few doors along the balcony from us lived my nan and grandad. My nan's sister, Auntie Jinny, also lived with them. Today we would say that she had special needs. In those days descriptions were less generous. Jinny used to keep budgies that spoke in a chirpy imitation of her own rather strange voice.

She once said to me, 'I had three budgies. But they both died.'

If you think my family was some kind of oddball anomaly, then think again. That block of flats was like the Twin Peaks of East London.

There was one chap who rejoiced in the handle Ol' Bollock Neck. Okay, 'rejoiced' may be pushing it. I expect he hated said moniker. But that is what everyone called him, either way. If you have a spare moment or two, I'd like to tell you about him, because if I don't, no one else will.

His given name was Reuben. He must have had a second name, but I never stumbled across it. I only knew he was Reuben because my mum, a woman of some natural refinement, refused to say the word 'bollock'. She said a lot of other things, but a bollock never crossed her lips.

Now Reuben was an unusual-looking chap, to be sure. Rotund and walking with a cane, he boasted the kind of bright-scarlet complexion that I now know indicates high blood pressure. Back then I just thought his head was about to explode. On top of that was a shiny bald pate on which sat three different-sized growths in close proximity to one another. From an aerial view, his dome must have resembled a small map of the Galápagos Islands. Such bumps on the nut were not uncommon back in the day. My dad's sister Eva had a couple we used to see every Christmas when we dropped off the presents. Having an – albeit thinnish – head of hair in which to conceal them gave Auntie Eva the drop on Reuben. But us kids would stay amused for hours trying to catch the occasional glimpse of one through her wispy backcombed barnet.

Good times.

Now, any or all of these physical attributes might have warranted the issuing of a nickname. But none were responsible for Reuben's. That, you may not be surprised to learn, was down to a goitre on his neck. And what a goitre it was. It hung down on his shirt collar like a honeydew melon ensconced in an XXL scrotal sack. The bastard thing was enormous.

Every time Reuben walked through the flats some budding cockney Oscar Wilde would shout out, 'Oy, Bollock Neck' in his general direction. For years his response would be to raise his cane in anger. Later, like a stone floor worn down by the passage of time, the same gesture became more of a tired acknowledgement.

Now I would never see Reuben or his bollock neck again.

There were others. Ginger Sadie on the ground floor, who had the misfortune to own a front room whose outside wall was the perfect size and location to serve as goal during our not infrequent kickabouts. The endless pounding of ball against brick must have driven her insane. The game would stop as she came out screaming the odds at us. Then resume again the second she walked back in. The sheer repetition of this scenario playing out was a comfort I would miss. Though I doubt Ginger Sadie felt the same.

And let's not forget Roughy Brian, the wiry teenage bully with perhaps the campest nickname in all East London. As an eleven-year-old, I had grown tired of him always pushing us around and finally decided to fight back. During the set-to that ensued, I bit him hard on the ear and pushed him down a flight of stairs. I became hero for a day and brought proof to the old adage about standing up to bullies. The day after that, Brian got an older mate of his to kick the crap out of me, and normal service was resumed. I never trusted an adage again from that day to this.

Now it was on to pastures new. And pastures there certainly were. Despite its East London postcode, North Chingford was remarkably rural, the more so to an inner-city slicker like my good self. There were fields and forests, a village green and cows that wandered freely in the streets. I used to tell my kids that the first time I set eyes on a cow I thought it was the biggest dog I'd ever seen. This was a joke. I'd seen pictures of them in books, obviously.

The main thing that struck me about Chingford was how

white and English it was. I had grown up amongst four-by-twos, Jamaicans, Irish and Pakistanis. The Jamaican presence, especially, had been impossible to ignore. The ska and blue-beat blaring out from the houses on Sandringham Road, the stalls selling exotic-looking fruit and veg down Ridley Road Market, the gaggles of snappily dressed rude boys hanging around street corners, talking in rapid-fire patois. It was a culture I took to easily and it had quickly left its mark. Queueing up for the latest Trojan releases in Musicland on Ridley Road Market. Playing them full volume on my sky-blue Dansette portable as I picked out my outfit for that night. The quiet thrill of being one of the few white faces in the Four Aces Club in Dalston.

Chingford was just a twenty-minute train ride away, but it may as well have been another planet.

I also made the mistake of arriving there with a bloated sense of self-importance. While I was still very young, I was a suedehead out of Hackney. One who had his new neighbours marked as yokels before he'd even met them. This misassumption was soon corrected. What they may have lacked in attention to sartorial detail, they endeavoured to make up for with an endlessly imaginative capacity for extreme violence.

There was a local night spot, the Lorraine Club, where such youths would gather for a skank and a punch-up. One night, a bus ferrying would-be revellers was attacked and firebombed by a rival mob from Debden. Seriously. Who firebombs a double-decker bus on a village green?

Another time I was at a dance at the Chingford Assembly Rooms when a Wild West-style fight broke out. Amidst the mayhem, a cassocked priest appeared with raised arms and appealed for peace. It didn't work. A fat bloke called Lips picked him up and threw him off a balcony. 'Seaside Shuffle'

9

by Terry Dactyl and the Dinosaurs was playing at the time. I've always had an ear for detail.

Being less than enthralled with this new environment, I would get the train back to Hackney most nights and hang out with my old mates. I'd then get a late train home to Chingford and make the twenty-minute walk to our flat, which was on The Ridgeway, near the fire station.

On one such journey, while walking along Station Road, I saw three skins, all older than me, hanging around the dark and otherwise deserted street ahead. I felt like the captain of the *Titanic* must have on first spotting a big chunk of ice through his binoculars. I knew there was going to be trouble, as you always do on such occasions. I put my hand inside the pocket of my Harrington and clenched my keys in my fist as a makeshift weapon. Then I kept walking. Closer, closer, closer . . .

'Wotchoo fuckin lookin at?'

Now I could have said, 'three ungainly troglodytes wearing the fashions of six months ago', or even, 'the excellent range of cycling accessories on offer in Halfords' window'. But discretion being the better part of valour, I elected to remain silent. It did me no good at all. They came and they came hard. I was battered senseless. Welcome to Chingford.

I arrived home a bloodied mess and my old woman immediately went into her world- famous impression of a hysterical Jewish mother. This was almost as painful as the beating. She repeatedly asserted that I must have done something to annoy them. Which is a very Jewish take on a random act of violence.

But in a way she was right. I didn't look quite like them. I didn't even walk like them. Like most of my mates, I'd picked up a bit of a Jamaican stroll, where you push yourself up on one foot as you go. It was an arrogant strut. One that could be quite annoying on a Jamaican, and a good deal more so on a fifteen-year-old Jewish kid. Either way, they had sensed I didn't belong and that had been enough.

My mum and dad, on the other hand, were settling nicely into their new upwardly mobile lifestyle. Away from the family, they had started to make new friends. Amongst these were our neighbours, the Joneses, who were both Welsh and schoolteachers. Moira, the missus, was lovely. In her early thirties, she had long brown hair and brown eyes, a fresh-faced smile and wore tiny cotton minidresses. She reminded me of a TV series of the time called *Take Three Girls*, about a flat-share in 'swinging London'. All I can recall about Mr Jones is that his name was Arfor and he had a beard – which probably tells you as much about me as you'll ever need to know.

The Joneses would often be invited in for dinner, which was of itself an innovation. Dinner parties? What the fuck? The nearest we'd come to such things in Hackney was when someone brought home a tin of pie and mash and we'd all gorge ourselves senseless, sat around the telly.

At these soirées it was always Moira who held court. She was bubbly and talkative and a fount of modern, progressive ideas. This was all new terrain to me, and I couldn't get enough. Of Moira, or her free-spirited ideals. She always made a point of talking to me like I was an adult and asking my opinions. Probably the first grown-up to ever do so. In return for such flattering generosity, I made her the regular star of my teenage sex fantasies for years to come.

I recall one time looking out of my first-floor bedroom window down at the back garden. Moira lay asleep on the grass and her dress had risen up around her waist. It was the most erotic thing I had ever seen. Though at that point in my development it would be fair to say competition was some-what thin on the ground.

When we moved, I'd switched schools from Hackney Downs to Sir George Monoux in Walthamstow. The two establishments had a lot in common. Both had delusions of grandeur rooted in their past. Both were shit-holes by the time I got there.

At Hackney Downs our official school sport had been a game called fives. It was played in something like a squash court, only with a padded glove and hard ball. The game had been invented by students at Eton in the late nineteenth century. What the fuck it was doing in Hackney in the late sixties was anyone's guess.

But Monoux managed to top even that. There we had all-year-round swimming lessons in the icy-cold school pool. Lessons in which all students were compulsorily naked. Imagine it. Forty-odd pallid teenagers stood trembling with cold and embarrassment, hands clasped over their bollocks, before being ordered down into the freezing water. The school's official line was that it was 'good for the constitution'. Personally, I could never see the connection between wellness and having your cock out.

As if all this was not sufficient a treat, our teacher, a boss-eyed geezer, name of Chatwin, would stroll around poolside with an 'ampton the size of an anteater's snout slapping about against his thigh as he went. Yup, he was also naked – despite never actually getting into the water himself.

Try putting that in an Ofsted report and see how far it gets you.

But it was at Monoux that I would eventually start to make new friends. My recent transition from hard-working student to class wag undoubtedly helped the process along.

'Name me two types of chemical bond.'

'Premium and James?'

'Get out.'

My best mate was Neal Weaver. He was into the same clothes and music as me, and also a Spurs supporter. We started going over White Hart Lane together and then hanging out of an evening. Neal was a star player for the school football team and had a kind of Prom King gloss about him. Neither of these things were remotely true of my good self, so knocking about with him helped put me on the fast track to a new social circle.

Another advantage was his sister Jacky. She of the Twig the Wonderkid eyes and immaculate dress sense. She and her crew of mates were as sheepskin-coated goddesses. Older, cute and very cool. I was in awe of them.

It was Jacky who first mentioned the Tottenham Royal dance hall to us. In its time the Royal had been a haunt of Teddy boys and, later, mods. Bands like the Who and the Dave Clark Five had also played there. Now it was once again the place to see and be seen. Truth be told, we'd never heard of it. But we acted as though we had, then headed down there at the first opportunity.

From the moment I set foot on that hallowed ground, I knew the Royal was a game-changer. It was cavernous, there were disco balls and it had plastic palm trees. Most of all, it was full of kids like us from all over London, all dressed up to the nines. I was in heaven.

Years later I would write about the Tottenham Royal in my song 'Saturday Night Beneath the Plastic Palm Trees'.

> *'69 was a very fine year*
> *Was a teenage rebel who knew no fear*
> *Hanging around the flats at night*
> *Drunk on cider, out of sight*

Six months later, barnet's grown
I got a mohair suit to call my own
Button-down shirt with a window-pane check
Brand new strides with a dogtooth fleck

Growing up, I need much more
Youth club kids were such a bore
Me mate Neal says there's a place he knows
Where his elder sister and her mates all go

Saturday night beneath the plastic palm trees
Dancing to the rhythm of The Guns of Navarone
Found my Mecca near Tottenham Hale Station
I discovered heaven in the Seven Sisters Road

Crews from Balham and Golders Green
And loads of places I've never been
The stroke of ten, a fight breaks out
Hear the bouncers scream and shout

Sling him out, he's wearing boots
Cry the gangsters dressed in dinner suits
They black his eyes, his nose gets bent
Courtesy of the management

Saturday night beneath the plastic palm trees
Dancing to the rhythm of The Guns of Navarone
Found my Mecca near Tottenham Hale Station
I discovered heaven in the Seven Sisters Road

Eddie Holman slows things down
You ask a girl to dance, but you get turned down
Maybe it's just not your day
What d'you want for five bob, anyway

I was cool, drinking rum & black
And then felt sick on the journey back
I got soaked right through in the pouring rain
But next week I'm going back again

Saturday night beneath the plastic palm trees
Dancing to the rhythm of The Guns of Navarone
Found my Mecca near Tottenham Hale Station
I discovered heaven in the Seven Sisters Road

'Seven Sisters Road' was a bit of artistic licence. It was further down, on Tottenham High Road. But that would have made a really shit chorus.

What was great about our nights out at the Royal was that my old mates from Hackney would also be there. So I'd spend my time flitting back and forth between my two groups of friends. After a while, I'd spend less time with the old crew. It was a little like getting together with someone you'd met on holiday. Without that thing you'd had in common, there just wasn't much to talk about. Eventually, the night came when I didn't even bother going over to say hello.

I'd relocated to Chingford with my parents some eighteen months before. Now, finally, I had moved.

EVEN ANDROGYNOUS CREATURES OF THE NIGHT ARE PRONE TO PAINFUL WARDROBE INJURIES

The years 1971 to 1972 brought many changes. Most of which were to my wardrobe. I had gone from monogram-blazered, Dapper Dan suedehead to East London's very own Spider from Mars. Neon-ginger electric-shock hairdo, eye make-up, bright blue Mr Freedom Oxford bags and Anello & Davide girls' shoes. At a strapping six foot two, I did not blend into crowds easily.

By this time, I also had a regular girlfriend, whom we'll call Hazel. Hazel wasn't her real name. But the lady in question is now married to a vicar and I have no wish to cause her any embarrassment or trample over her old man's sacraments.

Hazel was what we used to call a top sort. Also a former suedehead, she was now all pillbox hats, huge purple quiff and Miss Mouse skin-tight pencil skirts. Together we looked like we'd just left a party at Warhol's Factory and were on our way to meet Bryan Ferry for cocktails.

But in truth we were guttersnipes. Council-flat kids living

at home with our parents. And as such there was one thing we valued every bit as much as tickets to see Ziggy at the Rainbow or a day out shoplifting at Biba. That most priceless commodity for young couples since records began. *Time alone indoors*. Because in those days working-class parents barely left the house unless it was to bring back provisions. The world we aspired to was all bisexual creatures of the night taking a walk on the wild side. But in Manor House N4 I had to make do with a quick kiss goodnight on the doorstep while I tried to slip my hand inside Hazel's bra before her dad came out. And Hazel's dad always came out. Many's the time I walked home with balls the same colour as my Oxford bags.

So, when the lovely Hazel announced that her parents were going out to visit her brother and his wife, this was the cause of some celebration. Cue Bowie boy clicking wedge heels together while performing a Lindsay Kemp-inspired dance of joy in the front room.

On said day the parents did indeed exit as scheduled. I know this because I could see them through the bush I was hiding behind. I knocked on the front door and some thirty seconds after that, me 'n Haze are in bed.

Now it is a strange and, I think, indisputable truth that whatever point two people have reached in the gamut of sexual contact, the simple sound of a key entering a lock will bring all proceedings to an immediate and crashing halt. And so it was on this occasion. Hazel's parents came back. Apparently, they'd forgotten something. Like her old man's well-founded lack of trust in me.

I shot out of bed and, forgetting the niceties of underwear, was into my jeans in record time. But the manoeuvre did not go as planned. The meeting of an abruptly softened penis and a harsh metal zipper was never going to be a warm one with greetings exchanged. But the surge of unbridled agony that

18

coursed through my lower region was indescribable. White Light/White Heat/Blue Murder.

You remember that little metal spiky bit that used to be at the base of zips? *That.* I was well and truly speared. Worse still, the only position I could find any relief in was bent over double. So that was how I stayed. Tears now streaming down my face. Hazel tried to help. But it was useless.

Her mum got wind of the situation and proved to be an unexpected ally. First she kept the old man at bay. Then she entered the bedroom clutching a pack of Lurpak – slightly salted, as I recall – and offered a helping hand. I declined. The prospect of a sixty-year-old Jewish woman basting my old chap like a miniature Christmas turkey was doing nothing for my rapidly fading dignity.

I can't say who it was that eventually called for an ambulance. But I have a vivid recollection of two paramedics trying and failing to stifle laughter.

'Grit your teeth and I'll give it a quick rip upwards,' said one. 'Like fuck you will,' I replied politely.

And so I was lifted onto a stretcher – sitting bolt upright – and carried out into the lift. Which had people in it, *of course.* The ambulance ride that followed wasn't much fun either. It's amazing how aware one can become of uneven road surfaces in that position.

We arrive at hospital and I'm thankfully whisked straight through for immediate treatment. Even today the National Health charter ensures all A & E departments have a policy of prioritising embarrassing penis injuries.

The steady stream of giggling young nurses who poke their heads around the curtain is the stuff of nightmares. But that's a prelude to the doctor who approaches, wielding a razor-sharp scalpel inches above my crotch.

'Try and relax,' he says. This is not so easy, considering

the last time anyone went near my penis with a scalpel a significant slice of foreskin ended up down the waste disposal.

He comes in closer ... closer still ...

And begins to cut away my jeans. I breathe a huge sigh of relief. In around a minute I am naked from the waist down. Only with a zip hanging off my knob.

Without the encumbrance of the jeans, he is soon able to release my now battle-weary member.

Free at last, free at last. Thank God I'm free at last.

I'm left with what was then known rather unpleasantly as a black man's pinch. A distorted bubble of blackened blood under the skin.

'Can I give you anything for that?' asks my saviour.

'Do you have anything that'll ease the pain but keep the swelling?' I enquire. He doesn't laugh. I leave.

Which might be a good place to end this sorry tale. Save for one thing.

I had to walk back out onto the street to get the bus home. With my Ziggy haircut, no shoes, a shirt Hazel had thoughtfully draped around my shoulders and a pair of jeans that had the crotch cut out. And no underwear.

And that, my friends, really was a walk on the wild side.

A MAN CALLED ALF

Walthamstow Town Hall is a handsome devil of a building that I'm never less than happy to cast my minces upon. Designed and built by British architect Philip Dalton Hepworth in 1942, it's set way back from the road, with clean lines constructed from white-grey Portland stone. It also boasts a beautiful fountain-cum-water feature out front.

Increasingly, as the years tally up, things I'm drawn towards tend to have memories attached to them. Well done, Geoff, you're finally turning into your mother. Anyway, such is the case with the Town Hall. Be it sitting with my kids, cooling our feet in the water during a scorching hot summer gone by or warming up with a glass of mulled wine from my buddy Bruno's stall during the annual Christmas market. So not just a good-looking gaff, then. A happy one.

Inside the Town Hall are the beautiful Art Deco Assembly Rooms. In the early seventies I had a part-time job working as a kitchen porter for a caterer named Alf Altmann. The weddings and bar mitzvahs Alf catered were usually held at the Assembly Rooms, so it became home turf. Remember that stupid-looking bloke with the dyed Bowie cut, loading heavy tea chests full of crockery and kitchen equipment onto a truck while you were waiting around in your finery for your carriage to take you home? That was yours truly. Those Mr Freedom Oxford bags didn't pay for themselves.

Working for Alf was long, hard and frugally rewarded. A seventeen-hour day for a score and a roast chicken. But as I had no discernible skill set beyond an ability to turn up, I didn't much grumble. Truth be told, I enjoyed it. The people were friendly, and we had a laugh. And being part of a well-drilled if somewhat frenzied operation was strangely satisfying. These functions were huge life events for the people hosting them, and there was a genuine desire not to let them down.

At the centre of proceedings, barking out orders like Monty at El Alamein, was the always irrepressible Alf. Alf looked in his early seventies but with the stress his chosen field inspired, he could have been thirty-two for all I know. He'd kick off the day by sending me out to get his cigarettes. One hundred Senior Service. Untipped. Yikes. By eight in the evening, he'd run out and was poncing off others. For most of the day, you wouldn't see Alf. You'd just hear his unmistakable rasp emerging from behind a dense cloud of smoke. A one-man Chernobyl in a tux that had seen better days.

But Alf knew the game inside out. And what a game it was. A cycle of cooking, plating up, serving, clearing away, washing up and then going again. Through six courses for around 250 to 300 people. Plus canapés, champagne cocktails and a cold buffet on arrival.

Not to mention a bar fully stocked and manned for the endurance. Did I mention the coffee and pastries served later in the evening? Just in case the 17,000 calories previously consumed had been burned up on the dance floor.

Things would go wrong. Sometimes disastrously so. Rock-hard sorbets, split sauces, ovens that wouldn't heat. On one occasion a chef cracked under the pressure and did a runner mid-service. But Alf was wired into the entire event like Davros to the Dalek empire, and a solution was always close to hand.

At the end of the night, the guests having left happy, Alf would survey the now empty ballroom, point to the tables, and bellow out his inevitable, final order of the day.

'Fruit off, flowers off, fuck off.' And we did.

ADVENTURES IN
THE RAG TRADE

There seemed to be a lot of characters about when I was growing up. Maybe there still are. Or maybe there isn't sufficient
breathing space for them to thrive any more. I'm not sure. I
remember my late cousin Tony, a black cabbie of the Gooner
persuasion, telling me about another driver whose entire
raison d'être had been to secretly slip items of cutlery about
the person of others he ran into in the course of his working
day. So one might stop to exchange pleasantries, then arrive
home to find a fork and spoon secreted away in your over-
coat pocket. Kept it up for a lifetime, apparently. I've always
admired that kind of commitment to a cause. Especially when
it's a stupid one. Anyway, enough bunny. Here are a few words
on one such character of my historic acquaintance.

Back in the day – we're talking 1973 or thereabouts – I had
a Sunday job working down Brick Lane for a legend of a
geezer with the unlikeliest of handles, Sefton Cheskin. What
to say about Sefton? A four-by-two in his mid to late forties,
he sported a dodgy auburn syrup worn at a rakish angle
and was an inveterate *spieler* on a losing streak the length of

the Yangtze. Sefton owned a run-down old shop that was stuffed to the rafters with piles of clothes, mostly whistles of every size, shape and colour. Little was in any semblance of order and nothing was priced. It was a smallish gaff, but of a Sunday, Sefton had some ten or twelve youngsters like me working for him. Most of the boys were Jewish and worked during the week at esteemed West End establishments such as Cecil Gee and Take 6.

So what attracted us all to a madhouse like Cheskin's? In short, the money and the larks. For this was a shop like no other. Well, no other I've ever happened across. The day would kick off with Sefton arriving with a tray of warm Chelsea buns fresh from Kossoffs baker's, their sweet, cinnamon aroma filling the air. The chaps would stand around tucking away the pastries and drinking coffee until the first customers arrived. Which rarely took long. And when they came, it was usually thick and fast. But here's the thing. Sefton's clientele was almost exclusively Nigerian, usually wanting to bulk buy at a discount to take home to flog. Try to visualise it. A cramped shop full of unpriced *schmutter* and back-to-back Jews and Nigerians haggling over price and quantity. It was like the fucking Somme in there. And all manner of attempted trickery from both sides was par for the course.

A lot of the whistles in Cheskin's were actually very good. Probably retailing straight for about a ton to £120, even in those days. Others looked like they'd been knocked up by a blind Bulgarian working out the back of a hooky polyester farm. These were not worth the price of a stale Scotch egg. So if you could slip one of the latter into a purchase of a dozen of the former, you and Mr Cheskin would be quids in, even after having had some outrageous, last-minute discount beaten out of you by the punter. That was how the game worked. No rules, and fuck off will I take a Gregory Peck. Readies only, mate.

I remember one time Sefton bought in a job lot of about a hundred or so greatcoats. The kind of thing that was popular amongst students and hippies at the time. Nigerians, not so much. And to make matters worse, they were a fifty-six-inch chest. Every fucking last one of them. But if you could out even one, the *buntz* would be significant, what with Sefton Cheskin having picked them up for a price in the vicinity of *gornisht*. If you could cajole a punter into trying one on – 'Just in from Paris. Exclusive. And I can do you a deal' – you still had to get around the fact they were some ten sizes too big. To overcome this, we would explain that being the height of contemporary fashion, the way to wear them was belted at the back. We would assist with this, folding in ruddy great swathes of excess greatcoat behind the belt in the process. Coats were sold, money was made, and many laughs were had.

But the most memorable thing about working for Sefton Cheskin Esq. was the man himself. Every conversation I ever had with him or saw him have with anyone – be it friend, employee or punter – was littered with references and asides to 'Mrs McArdle': 'That looks lovely on you, mister. Mrs McArdle was in yesterday – she bought one for her Harold. He was happy, but I bet her Bert will have something to say. Ooh, look there she is now. Mrs McArdle . . . Gotta go, mister, the young fella will take your money.'

Needless to say, Mrs McArdle didn't exist. Unless she was a distant relative of Larry Grayson's Everard. It was just Sefton's thing. How it started and why he did it I couldn't really hazard a guess. I'd like to say people just did shit like that back then. But they didn't really. It was only him.

*

NB. Months after writing this, I was having a chat with a latter-day mate of mine, Mark Baxter, and it turned out Bax had also come across the man Sefton. Back in 1989, the week the Berlin Wall had come down, they had run neighbouring stalls in Camden Market. As luck would have it, not too far away from an old building that was being demolished. At Sefton's bidding, Bax had decamped to said building and returned with a sack full of rubble. The two of them then proceeded to make a killing, flogging its contents to unsuspecting tourists as 'genuine pieces of the Berlin Wall'. Back then, you see, you really could be heroes just for one day.

THE MILLION-POUND MOD
AND MY JUST DESSERTS

It might surprise you to learn that I went to law college. It may surprise you a little less to learn that I only lasted three weeks. It was perhaps the greatest mismatch since *Playboy* model Anna Nicole Smith's honeymoon night with 89-year-old billionaire J. Howard Marshall.

And definitely less fun to watch.

How did I end up there? Parental pressure, mostly. Well, entirely. I'd left school with next to no qualifications, thanks to my burgeoning devotion to clothes, music and a bit of a social, but I had managed to pick up three good A levels at North-East London Poly. This despite the fact that I rarely attended lectures and had spent most of my time playing poker or table football and chasing around after girls. It turns out if you're happy to read stuff, which I always am, some of it stays in your head. Who knew?

I didn't have a clue what I wanted to do with my life – still don't, for that matter – so my folks persuaded me that if I qualified as a lawyer in the meantime, I'd always have that to fall back on. I'm pretty sure I could see the flaws in that argument, even then. But my mum in full flow was like a

passive-aggressive tsunami with a Ph.D. in emotional manip-
ulation. I had neither a viable alternative nor the energy to
resist.

Sitting in lectures with my Ziggy haircut, three earrings
and a baggy plastic mac I'd picked up from Laurence Corner
surplus stores on the Euston Road, it didn't need a Pinkerton's
detective to work out that I didn't fit in with the Hooray
of Henrys in their tragic three-piece whistles that were my
fellow students. But in truth, my fate was sealed before I even
entered the building.

The college, at Lancaster Gate, was a straight run down the
Central line from Redbridge, where we now lived. As I was a
potless student, my mum had bought me my train pass. What
I did not know was that back then such passes came with a
code which signified the gender of the purchaser. These were
simpler times, you understand. Today you'd need to resurrect
Alan Turing to cover all those bases.

So it was that on my first day at law college I came through
the station wielding a woman's train pass. The ticket inspector
thought I'd half-inched it and stopped me at the gate. I tried
explaining but he wasn't having it. I was already nervous and
as the seconds ticked away, the prospect of being late made
it worse. Starting to panic, I ever-so-gently brushed the
inspector aside and walked on briskly with my head down.

At which point a do-gooder decides to intervene. 'I
saw that,' he bellows loudly while blocking my way. 'You
assaulted that man. I'm a witness. Call the police! Call the
police!'

This was just what I needed. His words were as Aladdin's
hand stroking the magic lamp. Only, instead of a genie
appearing, it was council-flat Geoff. Skinhead Geoff. Terraces
Geoff. And he was in no mood for granting wishes.

'Fuck off,' I counter eloquently, delivering a hefty shove

for dramatic emphasis. I then bid them all a fond adieu and exit hot-foot to college.

As I'm sat there trying to compose myself and not look as out of place as I feel, my lecturer enters. It's the do-gooder from the station. Our eyes meet but do not otherwise exchange pleasantries.

I don't see this working out, I think to myself. Three weeks later I get up and walk out mid lecture, never to return.

Having some unexpected time to myself, I go for a stroll around Kensington to consider my future and have a gander at the many fine clothes shops in the locale. Mostly the latter, if I'm being honest.

Somewhat fortuitously, these two strands run in to each other and I end up getting myself a job at the John Stephen boutique in Kensington Church Street. I figure arriving home with a job might help break the fall when I tell my parents about the unexpected swerve in my (their) life plan. Epic fail as it transpires but that's strictly by the by.

Now John Stephen is a name I am already familiar with and quite excited by. Known as the 'million-pound mod', he was a hugely influential figure in men's fashion in the sixties and early seventies. He made clothes for the Kinks, the Who, the Stones and the Small Faces and his shops, such as Mod Male, Lord John and John Stephen, were amongst the first to introduce a previously suspect flamboyance into the male wardrobe. A working-class gay youth from Glasgow, Stephen had come to London at the age of eighteen and worked at Moss Bros, where he learned to cut patterns and sell clothes. Finding the company a tad starchy for his taste, he jumped ship and landed a gig at Vince in Newburgh Street, an altogether different kind of establishment. Vince was the pseudonym of Bill Green, a photographer who specialised in shooting wrestlers and bodybuilders in skimpy briefs for 'underground' men's magazines. Punters who bought the mags were apparently as taken with the underwear as their contents – this being the golden age of enormous Y-fronts – and wrote in asking where they could buy them. Bill began to moonlight as Vince, and the rest is retail history. They did a roaring trade, mainly to homosexuals and theatrical types and if anyone can tell me the difference in the late fifties, there'll be a signed copy of this tome winging its way to you at the earliest opportunity.

Somewhere between his Moss Bros training, flogging gear to uncatered-for niche markets and being a young, gay, working-class bloke, a coin dropped deftly in Stephen's grey matter. He opened His Clothes in Beak Street in '57 and immediately started experimenting with close-fitting silhouettes and garish fabrics never before seen in menswear. By 1966, with the cultural revolution of the Swinging Sixties at full pelt, Stephen had fourteen boutiques in Carnaby Street alone. That he had a huge impact on how young working-class men dressed in the UK and later around the world is a matter of fashion history. Come the revolution I shall sanction a statue in his honour.

There's a John Stephen yarn that I love, and although a little sketchy on detail, I shall share it anyway. After cracking away in London, Stephen opened a shop back in his hometown, where he was a popular man. Glaswegians, like many working-class communities, were proud of 'one of their own' who had done well for himself. But the city had a reputation for violent street gangs dating back to the 1800s, and in the sixties it often resembled a war zone when it kicked off between rival factions. During one such altercation, Stephen's shop was wrecked and its stock rifled. Being from the streets himself, he eschewed the assistance of the local constabulary and instead sought out a meet with the head of the Carlton

Tongs, the most ferocious of these gangs with a fearsome reputation. They came to 'an arrangement' that ensured his shop would come under the protection of the Tongs and from that day on no one ever bothered him or his staff again. You will not find such goings-on at the Westfield branch of River Island any time soon and personally, I think life is all the duller for it.

Despite all this, I didn't stay at John Stephen long. The sixties were over, and it seemed very staid compared to Tommy Roberts' pop-art clothing emporium Mr Freedom, further along the same road, with its Mr Feed'em basement eatery – which served up blue mashed potato and bowls of soup with plastic flies floating around in them – or Kensington Market, with its stack-heeled boots, velvet suits and patchouli ambience. I did get to meet John Stephen once. Immaculate and conservatively attired, he spoke in a camp, cockney Glaswegian accent and was accompanied by a big white dog named Prince. And yes, he pulled up in a Roller. Man had style.

Before I left his employ, I did manage to get myself into the kind of pickle that all too often seems to punctuate, if not perforate, my history. I think of it as my idiot gene. I had been in a relationship with a girl for some time, even though 'relationship' was not a word anyone cared to use back then. You were 'courting' or 'seeing a sort'. The sort in question was the lovely Hazel, who is mentioned elsewhere in these recollections. A young woman with a shiny mahogany bob who had been my regular companion from suedehead through to Bowie boy and had kept up with me every step of the way. No one wore Stirling Cooper or Miss Mouse like Hazel. She was a top sort.

But we had been together for years and were both very young and it's perfectly natural that at some point . . . actually,

I'm going to stop there. You know I'm about to plead clemency for the indiscretions that will follow, and hands up, I merit none whatsoever.

Which, as it happens, is exactly what I got. Just desserts will later be served in generous portions.

I had to undergo a short training period before starting work proper. During this time I met another trainee whom I shall call Paula. Not her real name – that was Janet – but no point embarrassing the woman unnecessarily. Paula was beautiful, slim, well dressed, with short brown hair and spoke with a working-class accent not a million miles from my own. Her breasts were like the Mona Lisa's eyes in as much as they seemed to follow me around the room. Paula and I hit it off big time and I fancied her in the way only a horny eighteen-year-old romantic born of an idiot gene could.

Now I should explain that me and my mates had a very rigid social curriculum back then. Certain nights we saw our girlfriends, most of the rest we'd see each other, and Sundays we'd stay in. Occasionally this routine could cause problems. Thursdays were reserved for girlfriends, but also a good night at the Room at the Top, Ilford's self-proclaimed 'premier night spot in the sky', set just behind Harrison Gibson furniture store. To give ourselves some leeway, every now and then myself, Dave and Brendan, my two best buddies, would prearrange to provoke an argument with our respective partners and storm out in faux anger. We'd then meet at 'The Rooms' at midnight and get in a couple of hours of boozing, *schmoozing* and dance-floor cruising before closing time.

With no mobile phones to track, message or call, or Instagram to record your whereabouts, it was out of sight, out of mind. What a time to be alive. For wayward teenagers and adulterers especially. I arranged my first date with Paula on a supposed 'lads' night' and out I jolly well snuck.

If I began the evening eager, I arrived home in the early hours besotted. Me, Paula and her pneumatic breasts had all got on famously. I couldn't wait to see her again.

But the course of true love never did run smooth specially when it's of the snaky, double-dealing variety. She didn't show up for our second date. I hung around for hours and went home crestfallen. I never actually had a crest, of course, but you get my drift.

Paula trotted out some excuse which I duly swallowed, but to cut a long story short, this became the template of our relationship. A sensational date after which I'd get stood up next time around. Sometimes she'd mix it up. I'd see her twice on the knock and then she'd not turn up the next three times. I don't know who coined the phrase 'treat them mean, keep them keen', but if they'd had a press launch for it, I'd have been the poster boy. I was in pieces. I couldn't eat, I couldn't sleep. The girl was driving me nuts. And should you be thinking that was no more than I deserved, let me assure you that my story has only just began.

One night, Paula asked me to pick her up at her home. I regarded this as a breakthrough of sorts, as we'd only ever met out before. However, when her mum opened the door and broke the news that she wasn't in, I realised it was business as usual. As I turned to leave, dejected, the nice lady took pity on me and invited me in for a cup of Rosy Lee, which I duly accepted. Teenage heartbreak being something of a thirsty business.

Mum explained to me that Paula had a boyfriend who was a right bad lot and did not treat her with any distinction what-soever. Mums being mums, you can guess what she thought of that. Paula would regularly split up with this no-good low life, but then he'd whistle and she'd go running back. My role in this tawdry soap opera had been as nattily dressed stopgap.

Mum had liked the sound of me and had tried to encourage her daughter in my direction. Little did she know, eh?

Mum was a divorcee and, it must be said, no slouch on the scenic front herself. If I'd taken the trouble to go and see *The Graduate* a few years earlier, the evening might have taken an altogether different turn. Now that would have complicated matters. As it was, I polished off my cuppa and a brace of chocolate fingers, bade her a very good evening and took my leave.

Later that night in my bedroom I sat down and wrote a letter to Paula. It was without doubt the single most embarrassing collection of words ever put together in sequence in the English language. Perhaps any language. I loved her, I could not live without her, and this other reprobate was not deserving of her many fine qualities. I did not say 'including your pneumatic breasts' because that would have ruined the tone, but instead went on to grovel, beg and implore her, at great length, to choose me. I didn't actually sign it 'the biggest wanker on God's green earth', but I didn't have to. It was all there in my words. My very many, horribly ill-judged words. The next day I bought a stamp and posted it, feeling sure it was only a matter of time until I'd be sweeping her up in my arms.

I don't want to get all Google Maps on your ass, but I need to talk a little geography because it plays a part in what happens next. Hazel, the regular girlfriend, lived in Manor House. Technically North London, but I always think of it as very upper Hackney. Paula lived in Waltham Cross, which was miles away in Hertfordshire. There was no reasonable way their paths would ever cross in many months of Sundays.

But I forget to factor in that Hazel has a brother some twenty years older than herself. Now I like Hazel's brother. He has a face like Mr Punch, the well-known glove puppet, and a personality gleaned from watching too many Marx Brothers movies. Despite being a grown- up with a successful business, one of his favourite party pieces is to kick posh-looking strangers up the arse in public places and then stand around looking wistfully innocent. I see him pull off this ruse many times and never once does it fail to coax a smile. Mr Punch also has a mate called Wadey who once bought a lion which he kept around the house but that's a story for another day.

Anyway, it's a few days since I sent my letter and I've heard nothing back from Paula. Hazel calls me on the dog and bone and tells me she's decided to stay with her brother and his wife for the weekend. Good, I think. I can pace up and down frantically in peace. But here comes the plot twist. It does not occur to me that Mr Punch and his good lady reside in Potters Bar. Which, as luck would have it, is also situated in the borough of Hertfordshire.

And so it came to pass that on the Friday night, Hazel and her sister-in-law Mrs Punch pop out to a local hostelry for a couple of sherbets. Here they find themselves standing along-side a large group of girls, one of whom is holding court and causing the others to collapse in peals of laughter. She does this by reading loudly from a letter she holds in her hand. Line by line, omitting not a word, from beginning to end. And there is enough character and detail in the wretched missive for Hazel to suss out that I am, in fact, its author. I mean, seriously. What are the odds?

I don't know what's worse. Getting caught out bang to rights and being thoroughly humiliated in the process. Or knowing that the chance of this happening must have been a billion to one, or thereabouts. But happen it did and suffer I would as a result.

Despite me blotting my copybook in such spectacular

fashion, Hazel did not end the relationship. Instead she elected to impale me on a spit of guilt and roast me over burning coals of shame on a daily basis for the rest of our time together.

Game, set and match to the lovely Hazel.

MUSIC WAS MY FIRST LOVE, ALONG WITH CLOTHES AND MY HAIR, OBVIOUSLY

Music was always important to me, but being in a band wasn't something that featured heavily on my to-do list. Not for years, anyway. I grew up in East London in the late sixties and, like most working-class kids from my manor, going out meant clubs and dance halls, rather than gigs. And music meant records. Not *pop groups*. It's an entirely different state of mind.

My music of choice in those days was ska and rocksteady, exquisite Jamaican *riddims* bequeathed to us by our mod antecedents. And when I say 'us', I mean skinheads, of course, though this is not a name I heard anyone use at the time. 'Pinheads' or 'peanuts' were descriptors bandied about on occasion, but by observers, not us.

We had a way of dressing, of wearing our hair, of dancing. But that was just the way we were. The fashion of the day. The skinhead tag would come much later. With the bleached-denim boneheads, the racism and the tabloid headlines. None of which had anything to do with the vibrant, multicultural movement I had known.

I'd had the odd flirtation with the worlds of rock and pop. At the age of ten I queued up for tickets to see the Beatles at the Walthamstow Granada with my cousin Denise, who was newly teenaged and already wearing miniskirts so short she was scared to move for fear of flashing her Jack and Danny at all and sundry. We waited in line for hours and eventually got our precious tickets for the Fab Four. I stashed mine in an orange teapot fashioned into the shape of a cottage that my parents used to file away all our important documents.

A few months later, I was sitting indoors on a Friday night when the dog and bone rang. I know it was a Friday because *Gideon's Way*, a police show with John Gregson, was on the box. It was Cousin Denise. She excitedly asked me what I'd thought of the Beatles. Not much, as it turned out, because I'd forgotten to go. I always had a lot on my mind, even as a ten-year-old.

In later life I was never a big Beatles fan. So much of the music I love is connected to times and places, my sense memory triggered by one tune or another. I sometimes wonder how things might have turned out if I'd made that show at the Granada instead of watching Inspector Gideon feel the collar of some 'erbert. But I didn't. So, whenever two mates are sitting in the pub arguing what was the better album, *Sergeant Pepper* or *Revolver*, I tell them *Tighten Up Volume 2* pisses over both and sidle up the ramp for another sherbet.

In 1968 I went to Hyde Park, where Blind Faith headlined a free open-air concert to a crowd of some 100,000. My outfit for this occasion was a light blue Oxford cotton Ben Sherman, a maroon sleeveless pullover, bronze Sta-Prest and a pair of DMs, which might lead you to question what had drawn one such as myself to an event of this nature. My pal

Gordon, who was older and knew about such things, had told us it would be full of hippies, and hippy women were renowned for taking off their shirts and dancing around topless at such shindigs. Seeing an erstwhile supergroup bash out some blues-based fusion nonsense had as much appeal as a rusty spike up the jacksy. But bare breasts were a different thing altogether. I was fourteen and desperate for my first sighting.

Sad to report not a solitary bristol was spotted that day, the English weather curbing the *esprit libre* of the flower generation. When the Edgar Broughton Band began chanting a chorus of 'out demons, out', me and my mates took it personally and slung our collective hook.

The first proper gig I went to was Desmond Dekker at the Four Aces, a ska club in Dalston, close to where I lived. As one of the few white faces in a packed house heaving with local rudeboys, it wasn't the most relaxed evening of musical appreciation I would ever spend. But Desmond sang all the tunes I knew and loved – 'The Israelites', '007', 'It Mek' – and I got home in one piece. Result.

Next was 'Little' Stevie Wonder at the Finsbury Park Astoria, which would later become the iconic Rainbow Theatre. When he was led out on stage, Stevie looked like a skinny, frail kid. But the second he started to perform, he grew into a man possessed. I'd never seen anything like it. By the time he launched into 'I Was Made to Love Her' everyone was out of their seats and dancing in the aisles. Unforgettable stuff.

Concert number three was the Four Tops, and with a hat trick like that I really should get to keep the match ball.

Truth be told, the Tops, with their matching suits and

perfectly choreographed dance routines, weren't strictly my cup of Rosie Lee. I was there because my mates were fans.

History seems to have forgotten that as many original skins and suedes were into Motown as they were into ska. Either way, seeing Levi Stubbs belt out '7 Rooms of Gloom' and 'Reach Out I'll Be There' was by no means any great hardship.

As good as these shows were, they dropped into my life from a different planet. All the artists were black, from Jamaica or the US. I was a working-class, Jewish kid from Hackney. So as far as inspiration goes, it was *nul points*.

There was no one musical in my family either. Not unless you count all the cab drivers tooting their horns at other road users for having the audacity to well, use the road.

My old man had a collection of Lonnie Donegan records he'd play now and again. I didn't mind those, as they were quite funny. There was one called 'Putting on the Style' where Lonnie randomly shouts out the word 'socks'. That always amused me, and I would sometimes join in. But I wouldn't count shouting out 'socks' as a calling.

My main musical recollections, family-wise, were sing-alongs at parties. Flanagan and Allen, old wartime tunes, the occasional music-hall ditty. There's something about working-class people coming together and singing that I've always loved. It's in my DNA. It's not hard to see why I was a huge fan of Chas & Dave. If they'd hailed from anywhere else in the world they would have been revered as indigenous folk musicians of the highest order.

My nan, who was a big, bold slice of East End woman-hood, used to organise coach trips to the seaside for herself and her cronies. She'd call them 'charabanc outings'. Both my parents worked, and I was often in Nan's care, so I would go along. Released from the constraints of domesticity for the day, these women were a joy to be amongst. The minute the coach pulled away, the singing would start, and it would not stop until the destination was reached. No sleep till Margate. 'It's A Long Way to Tipperary', 'Maybe It's Because I'm a Londoner', 'Pack Up Your Troubles', 'Daddy Wouldn't Buy Me a Bow-Wow'. You name it, they sang it. My nan's party piece on these trips would be to dance up and down the aisle of the coach – no health and safety in those days – singing her own version of Charles Coborn's old music-hall song 'Two Lovely Black Eyes'. The lyrics of the original are genuinely witty. They're about a man who's constantly getting into fights for expressing his political views.

The underlying moral is to never discuss politics, and it's possibly the only song ever to namecheck William Gladstone. Its chorus went like this:

> *Two lovely black eyes*
> *Oh, what a surprise*
> *Only for telling a man he was wrong*
> *Two lovely black eyes*

Nan's rendition differed somewhat:

> *My lovely red drawers*
> *My lovely red drawers*
> *There's a hole in the middle where I do a piddle*
> *My lovely red drawers*

To complement her performance, Nan would hoist her dress up around her waist to reveal a pair of long red-silk bloomers. The other women would whoop and holler and laugh hysterically. Nan lapped up the attention. Maybe I did inherit something from her.

School had done nothing to nurture my love of music. Music lessons consisted mainly of being made to sit quietly for an hour while our teacher 'Paedo' Williams, a brilliantined vulture of a man, force-fed us classical pieces via a shitty mono record player. If 'Paedo' caught your attention wandering, he'd viciously rap you over the knuckles with a violin bow. The pain was excruciating, and the irony of a music teacher using an instrument to deal out physical punishment entirely lost on him. I have no idea if he was really a paedophile, but he was definitely a cunt of the highest order.

Before leaving school, I had a five-minute interview with a careers officer. My O-level results had been somewhat disappointing, perhaps due to the fact I'd done most of my revision sitting beneath a plastic palm tree at the Tottenham Royal dance hall, genning up from 'key fact' cards while sipping nonchalantly on a rum and blackcurrant. The facts on the cards turned out not to have been very key to the bloke who set the exams. I messed up.

Royally, as it were.

Surveying my tawdry results, the careers officer didn't even bother to look up, and grunted just two words: 'Civil Service.' What possessed him to make such a recommendation I cannot fathom. I didn't know what the civil service was, and never bothered to ask.

The first band I ever saw that tapped into working-class culture and really spoke to me was the Faces. When Rod Stewart kicked a football into the crowd, he scored with every council-flat kid in the house. He was one of our own. The well-cut velvet suits, the trouble he took with his barnet. Rod the Mod's credentials were as plain as the not-inconsiderable nose on his deuce and ace. Jagger may have been a great frontman, but he was a middle-class boy. The Stones were sex and heroin and social revolution. The Faces were shagging and boozing and Sunday-morning markets. For me, 'Maggie May' and 'Stay With Me' were the soundtrack to 1971.

The immediate impact of Rod Stewart on my life was not to inspire me to start a band but to get my hair looking like his. For years, maintenance of my barnet had been taken care of by a gentleman who rejoiced in the handle One-Eyed Monty from Mare Street. Despite being somewhat underendowed in the mince-pie department, when it came to the intricacies of a number-one crop with razored-in side parting, One-Eyed Mo's aim was both straight and true. There was no finer barber this side of Seville. The man was a legend.

He was also a rather comfortably-off legend. This had little to do with his deft touch with a razor but owed much to his sideline of selling *shneid* National Insurance stamps to the local cabbies, knocked-off dresses to their wives and just about anything else he could lay his mitts on. Monty was the original one-stop shop. Something for every citizen. So much so, the local authorities decided to recognise his entre-preneurial endeavours on behalf of the community. He got five years for receiving and selling stolen goods.

With Monty out the picture and my hair now longer, it was time to venture into the brave new world of the West End hairdressing salon.

I arrived at Vidal Sassoon in South Moulton Street clutch-ing a handful of pictures showing Rod's barnet at its most perfect, and micromanaged my *stylist* through every snip of my new look. In fairness to him, when it was still wet it wasn't far off. Unfortunately, when my hair's longer, it's quite thick, with a wave, and after it dried, I wound up looking more like the bloke from Chicory Tip. No one wanted to look like the bloke from Chicory Tip. Not even him. That summer, every time I turned up anywhere my mates would greet me by singing the synth intro to the Tip's big hit, 'Son of My Father'.

I needn't have worried. Within a mere twelve months, music and my world – barnet included – will have been turned upside down by the cosmic sledgehammer that was the arrival of Bromley's finest son, one Mr David Jones. Bowie to his friends.

Like Rod, Bowie started out a moddy London boy with a hankering for rock and roll who wanted to be famous. But the likeness ended there. Bowie, it turned out, had a multitude of hankerings. He was into all sorts and gobbled up influences like a cultural Pac-Man. After a succession of false starts, he pulled it all together and re-emerged with the seminal *Ziggy Stardust* album, casting himself in the leading role. And if the significance of that is lost on you, you're probably reading the wrong book. Bowie changed everything. For my generation he was pop culture's ground zero. It wasn't just the music, which was expansive and magnificent, or the lyrics, which were like nothing I'd ever heard. It was the whole package. The neon ginger hairdo, the make-up, the clothes and, of course, the much-publicised bisexuality. I don't think I'd even heard the word bisexual before. And suddenly here was Bowie, married to a girl who looked as striking he did, talking freely of his affairs with men, going down on Mick Ronson's guitar on stage, and camply throwing his arm over the guitarist's shoulder on *Top of the Pops*. The sexuality of a nation's youth was kicked high into the stratosphere and would never be quite the same again. Parents scratched their heads in bemusement or outright hated him. Which of course only served to further endorse the credentials of the new messiah.

I had a friend, Kenny. A devout Bowiephile of the highest order. He turned up at our house, distraught, on Xmas Day. His dad, in a gesture of seasonal goodwill, had thrown him out of the house for 'looking like a queer'. My own parents' life experience was extremely limited, but they were relentlessly liberal when it came to treating people kindly and equally. He was invited to spend the day with us. What a Xmas lunch that was. Three four-by-twos and my mate Kenny, in a leopard-skin swagger jacket, with his hennaed hair, eye make-up and an array of gaudy bangles dripping from either wrist. Despite this, conversation did not stray far from the bounds of the usual, and we all put on party hats and pulled crackers. At one point my mum, perhaps beginning to entertain the wild notion that Kenny and I might be more than just good friends, leaned over and quietly whispered the $64,000 question into my ear.

'Is he Jewish?' she asked.

A real one-off, my old woman.

If Bowie headed the vanguard, on his flank was Roxy Music, led by a former fine-art student from Newcastle, Bryan Ferry. Like Bowie, Ferry's passion for a myriad of musical genres was enhanced by his broader artistic sensibilities. But the end results could not have been more different. After many hit-and-miss years in the music biz, the Ziggy album saw Bowie and the Spiders arrive fully formed. When Roxy exploded onto the scene, they were very much a work in progress. The Spiders were comprised of the rock-solid rhythm section of bass player Trevor Bolder and drummer Woody Woodmansey, which provided a foundation for the virtuoso guitar-playing of the marvellous Mick Ronson. Roxy's line-up on their first album included classical musician Andy Mackay on oboe and sax and Brian Eno twiddling the knobs and dials on his synthesisers, providing atmospheric, aural soundscapes, as well as an array of beeps and noises. If the Spiders were the perfect three-piece rock combo, Roxy were barely rock at all. Their sound was wildly experimental.

That difference runs right through the respective albums, which were both released the same week in 1972. Bowie was an experienced songwriter by the time he made *Ziggy*. He had already penned 'Space Oddity' and 'Life on Mars', two stone-cold, all-time classics. He was a man with a plan who knew exactly what he was doing. Every track on *Ziggy* is solid gold.

Roxy was new to the party and still trying shit out. The composition and structure of their songs could be bewildering. Bowie's magpie tendencies would eventually allow him to jump styles from one album to the next. Roxy would cram a myriad of influences into one song. They were retro, modern and postmodern all at once. To the fore and layering on the top line was Bryan himself, looking like space-age Elvis, sounding like a deranged, heavily mannered crooner. It could have, perhaps should have, been a disaster. But it wasn't. It was thrilling and riveting and beautiful. I had never heard anything like it in my life. No one had, because it didn't exist.

In truth, Roxy would never sound quite like this again. By the second album Eno had left, and Ferry and co. were quick learners. *Stranded*, while brilliant and unique, was forged within more traditional musical constraints. For me there is no more intriguing album on God's green earth than their first.

Amazingly, for such an avant-garde outfit Roxy received a lot of positive attention from the get-go. One notable exception was 'Whispering' Bob Harris, who at the time fronted the weekly *Old Grey Whistle Test* on the BBC. Unlike *Top of the Pops*, this was a show for 'serious' music fans. Bob himself was a laid-back dude with a penchant for country rock who never seemed to get much excited about anything.

But something about having Roxy guest on the show, *his show*, really stuck in Bob's craw. Maybe the array of lurex and leopard skin was too much for his denim-clad sensibilities. Or perhaps at some level he knew the jig was up. The new were coming and he and his hippy muso schtick were not a part of it. Either way, he introduced the band with a sneer and made a dig about 'style over substance', in doing so revealing his own myopic conservatism to the world. The man was so starved of true creativity he could not see it when it was right in front of his eyes. Roxy had style but exuded substance by the skip-load. Fuck you, Whispering Bob.

One thing Roxy Music of this period should not have been was a singles band. Yet due to the attention they were attracting, the record company wanted one. This unlikely combination of forces would lead to the one of the most remarkable pop records ever made.

'Virginia Plain' took all of the wit, innovation and craziness of Roxy's debut album, set it over a driving beat, and distilled it into two minutes and fifty-eight seconds of sheer joy. It eschewed everything a hit single was meant to be. Chorus? Nah, let's not. Yet somehow it was the perfect pop single. Along with Bowie's 'Starman' and Mott's 'All the Young Dudes' (also of course, penned by Bowie), they were my soundtrack of '72.

With two breakthrough acts exhibiting a fondness for dressing up and putting on make-up, others surely followed, and the press were quick to expand it into a movement which picked up the the that naffest of handles, 'glam rock'. There was Marc Bolan of course, who had transformed himself from hippy rockgoblin into pixie pop star, resplendent in satin and tat, and a star on his cheek. Bolan made some great records and I had soft spot for the man. Partly because in the not-too-distant past he had been Mark Feld, a young Jewish mod from Stamford Hill. 'The Hill', incidentally, was a four-by-two-heavy part of inner North London I'd knocked about in occasionally during my suedehead days. It was a lively manor, the social centre of which was a pinball arcade known as 'the schtip', the E & A Bar, which served delicious salt-beef sandwiches, augmented by a choice of two hot beverages, hot blackcurrant or lemon tea, and a bowling alley. What more could a young man want? Well, girls, obviously and the Hill had a surfeit of those too. Anyway, I digress . . .

The combined forces of glam were irresistible to young men such as myself. Bowie playing the Rainbow in '72 was a seminal life event. It was like an art-house fashion parade. Everyone there to see and be seen. I recognised a few faces from the Tottenham Royal. Their suedehead regalia, like mine, now long confined to the bin bags of history. The seedlings of both punk and the Blitz Kids movement were on parade that night. The fashion was less prescriptive than any I had known before, perhaps because nowhere yet sold the kind of clothes we wanted to wear. Tommy Roberts' magnificently innovative City Lights Studio – housed in a Covent Garden loft amidst the fruit warehouses – would attempt to fill that void later on in the year. For now, it was all about picking up the odd piece from shops like Cockell & Johnson in Kenny Market, or Alkasura in the King's Road, rummaging around second-hand shops – no one called them 'vintage' back then – and getting things made or altered.

A gang of us had gone to the Rainbow, including my best mates from North-East London Poly, David Jaymes and Brendan Keaney. Brendan was stick-thin, with an Irish twinkle in his eye, and a brilliant dancer. Fred Astaire with blue-black hair. He even carried a cane. Half-inched from Biba the previous week, if memory serves. Dave wore what looked like an old demob suit but with the trousers taken into a much narrower cuff. I'd gone for a pair of bright-yellow

Mr Freedom dungarees and a pair of square-toed shoes with three-colour platform soles I'd had made by Stan the Man of Walthamstow Market especially for the occasion. With the help of a bottle of orange hair dye, an array of products and some industrial-force blow-drying, my crowning glory was by now a reasonable approximation of the great man's. All in all, it would be fair to say we were not an understated ensemble. Dave and I also had attractive girlfriends who dressed very similarly – dyed hair, pillbox hats with veils, fox furs, skin-tight pencil skirts and impossibly high heels – which did much to enhance our group look.

But if I thought first prize for most impressive clothes horses was in the bag, I would be disappointed. A dude walked in with the exact same barnet and skeletal physique as Bowie. He wore a midnight-blue Lurex bomber jacket unzipped to the waist with nothing beneath it, striped pedal-pushers and knee-length red PVC boots with a huge black wedge heel. Identical to an outfit Bowie was wearing on this current tour and had recently been photographed in. How the fuck did he pull that off? If that wasn't enough, his companion was a fabulously turned-out dwarf girl.

Game, set and match to Little and Large.

The excitement generated by all this started me thinking about being in a band for the first time. Dave played bass with a local group. Brendan strummed a bit of guitar, and his old schoolfriend from St Ignatius, Kev Steptoe, was a highly rated young drummer. Could I sing?

I figured there was only one way to find out.

We began rehearsing in a room at college and, wonder of wonders, we sounded pretty good. Though in hindsight I've no doubt our enthusiasm eclipsed a multitude of shortcomings.

We arranged an in-house gig at the poly, which was not

difficult because Dave was social secretary and responsible for putting on events.

By this time, Dave and I had become thick as thieves. Surprising perhaps, because our backgrounds could not have been more different. He'd been educated at Forest, a local fee-paying school, and was the first middle-class person I'd ever really known. He'd clearly been through his teenage rebellion years because by the time we met he was wearing leathers and hanging out at the Bikers' House in Lea Bridge Road run by Buttons Walsh, the president of the UK Hells Angels. Buttons was a name I was already familiar with as a figure of note during the mods and rockers battles of the sixties. He'd risen to prominence after being shot in the chest outside Leyton Baths by a young modernist, name of Beardy Pegley. Personally, I think there must be easier ways of making a name for yourself.

Dave's associations with these people didn't impress me, perhaps because they were from the other side of the cultural divide. I used to take the piss out of him for it, which was not at all the look he was going for.

I was more intrigued by his middle-class trappings because that was all new to me.

We were both bright, but he knew about things I didn't. I suspect the same was probably true in reverse.

I recall one time in his house he was cooking pasta – itself not a common occurrence in home kitchens in the early seventies – when without warning, he threw some spaghetti against the wall. I thought the Hells Angels must have drugged him. Dave explained the concept of *al dente* to me and that if the pasta sticks, it's ready.

It was a long way from my mum's culinary style. The one time she'd made spaghetti, it was served on a plate with a pile of chips.

Dave also gave me tips on exam techniques. I didn't even know there were exam techniques. Without breaking much of sweat, my three shitty O levels were soon supplemented by three A levels at A grade.

But for now, education was on the backburner as our debut gig beckoned. We called ourselves Star, which is a rubbish name and I'm sure owed more than a little to Bowie.

The set was all covers. It hadn't occurred to us to try and write anything original. We played Roxy's 'Editions of You', The Velvet's 'White Light/White Heat', a high-camp version of 'Heartbreak Hotel', and Chuck Berry's 'Around and Around', amongst others. I wore a green metallic shirt which had absolutely no give in it and did not absorb any perspiration, matched with a pair of Mr Freedom Oxford bags. Their extreme width came in handy for the gallons of sweat cascading down into them. Brendan, who was always the centre of attention on the dance floor, was painfully shy on stage and spent the entire set with his back to the audience. Dave and I had no such reservations. Our musical talents may have been fledgling, but we preened and posed around that stage like champions. Behind us, Kevin's rock-solid drumming held everything together, just as it would years later in the Buzzards.

The crowd lapped it up and were dancing their arses off from the first number. Okay, it was a couple of hundred kids we knew from college. But what a buzz. Way more fun than the civil service. We decided there and then that this would be but the first step in our quest for world domination. Nothing, upon nothing, would stand in our way.

There was never a second gig. We carried on rehearsing for a bit and even started trying to write some tunes of our own, but then disaster struck. This particular disaster took place at a college disco, again at the North-East London Poly. As usual, Brendan was on the dance floor, all eyes on him, as he performed moves the rest of us couldn't even think about. Bren was a good-looking boy and attracted a lot of female attention. He was also dressed to the nines and wearing eye make-up. Any of these things could be enough to earn the resentment of a certain kind of person. All three were an open invitation.

There was gang of Greek lads at college. Older than us, macho, very old school. They didn't like the cut of Brendan's jib and, goaded on by the others, one of them went over to him and started taking the piss and pushing him around.

I saw what was happening. I was also dressed up and wearing make-up. But my provenance was a little more scrappy than Bren's. So, to cut a long story short, I introduced my forehead to the bridge of his tormentor's nose. It was not a happy meeting, and his bugle came off second best. He ran off.

Before I had so much as a second to bask in the afterglow of victory, a second figure appeared on the scene, and I knew straight away I was in trouble. He was shorter than me but as wide as he was tall. He'd removed his shirt to show off his muscled upper body. Even his muscles had muscles on them. And his whole torso was covered in a forest of thick, matted hair. It looked like pubic barbed wire. I could lose a hand even touching him. Before I'd had a chance to consider a course of action, he punched me hard on the chin. Harder than I'd ever been hit before. I instinctively put up my hands to defend myself, but his second blow landed on the side of my face and hurt just as much as the first. As the disco erupted into a mass brawl, I left without making my excuses.

There were some more fun and games outside, as my attacker had pursued me and was standing on one of the high grass banks that separated the college from the street, still shirtless, looking for me. By now I was in my car, about to drive myself to hospital to check out the damage. Sod it, I thought. In for a penny. I slammed my foot on the accelerator and headed up the bank.

If you happened to be walking along Forest Road, Walthamstow one night in 1973 and were bemused by the sight of a battered old Austin 1100 driven by a blood-soaked man in full make-up, chasing a stocky shirtless hirsute bloke around in circles on a grass bank, you now know the how and why.

At Whipps Cross Hospital I found out that those two punches had broken my jaw into three sections. To set it, they sewed my teeth together by threading metal wire through my gums with a needle. This hurt considerably more than the injury. I would now not be able to talk or eat properly for the next six weeks. To survive I had to drink Complan – a disgusting nutritional supplement made from skimmed milk and vegetable oil – and endless cans of Guinness. Can't imagine a doctor prescribing that these days. Either way, my career as a singer went on the back burner.

Soon after this our stint at college came to an end, and with it our rehearsal space.

New priorities loomed large in our lives. Finding work, earning money.

As we drifted towards the mid-seventies, it was also an exciting time socially and going out was a lot more appealing than sitting around rehearsing.

I remember one night Dave, Bren and I drove to the Goldmine in Canvey Island. DJ Chris Hill had introduced a swing night, which was huge fun. We'd dress up like American GIs and dance to the music of Glenn Miller, the Andrews Sisters and Louis Jordan. After a few hours we left and headed to Crackers in Soho, where DJ Mark Roman played obscure funk and was the best scene in the West End. The look at Crackers was very different, so we had a change of clothes in the boot. Peg trousers, mohair jumpers and plastic 'jelly' sandals. My thing was clear sandals worn with odd coloured socks. And if you think that makes me sound like a dick, it would be hard to present a compelling case for the defence.

The other thing that worked against taking the band more seriously was that there was no obvious way forward for us. The artists that we liked – Bowie, Roxy, Cockney Rebel *et al.* – were huge. They played big venues and put on lavish live shows. It seemed a lifetime away from anything we would or could ever be capable of. And popular as these acts were, there had been precious little trickle-down to the smaller gig circuit to inspire us.

One (kind of) exception was Ian Dury's Kilburn and the High Roads.

They certainly weren't glam, or anything close. But they were different. Strikingly so.

Self-styled 'Upminster kid', Dury had a pronounced limp, the result of a bout of polio as a child, and a unique way with words which was more akin to poetry infused with elements of old-time music hall than traditional song lyrics. The Kilburns' continually revolving door of members included artist Humphrey Ocean on bass, Guyanese born David Newton-Rohoman, who was the only drummer I ever saw who walked with crutches, and keyboard player Rod Melvin, who in later years would become a good friend.

For a time, the Kilburns were managed by the late Tommy Roberts, whose name crops up earlier in this story.

In matters of fashion, art and culture, Tommy was so far ahead of the curve he couldn't see it in his rear-view mirror. That he was an immaculately attired fat man with the demeanour of a talkative spiv made him all the more fascinating. The world became a duller place the day Tommy doffed his titfer and took his final leave.

Brendan and I loved the Kilburns and would always go and see them when they played in London, which was pretty much all the time.

Another band that attracted a fair amount of attention was Liverpool Art School refugees, Deaf School. Later, a whole generation of successful Scouse musicians would cite them as an influence. While I could see they were more interesting than most of what was on offer, I wasn't crazy about their music. Like the Kilburns, they struggled to make the transition from cult to mainstream success and eventually split up.

By 1975 all talk of the band had fizzled out. Brendan had become a contemporary dancer, a career he would excel at and loved. So we didn't even have a guitarist any more.

Dave and I were now working in a clothes shop in Leyton. A career with absolutely no prospects but one where we were left alone to get on with it and have a good laugh. Something which always carried a little too much weight with us both.

There had been one occasion when we were selling a wedding suit to a total melt and his intended. The trousers needed taking in around the seat, so Dave and I chatted to them about their coming big day in the dressing room while I knelt down and pinned them for him. After which he slipped them off. Unfortunately, I had accidentally pinned right through his underpants and as he pulled down his strides a big ginger knob jumped out at me, only inches from my face. This was too much. Dave and I were crying with laughter. Completely unable to compose ourselves as he struggled to unpin his pants with one hand and shield his member with the other.

That we still made the sale was a feat which far outweighed anything we would eventually achieve in our music careers.

The thing that ultimately rescued me from a future of humiliating unsuspecting customers was, of course, punk. But it was far from love at first sight.

Truth be told, I was a bit sniffy about punk at the beginning. I had my own shit going on. Grown-out wedge, skinny-fit suit, 'Let it Rock' painted tie, Warhol glasses and deadstock grey winklepickers from Levitt's down the Lane. I'd put in a lot of effort. Especially with those shoes, which were a size and a half too small for me. They looked good but I moved like a man with the worst case of Farmer Giles in medical history. Still, the notion of chucking out my wardrobe and trading in my record collection for some new movement seemed ridiculous.

Punk – with its fashion and art school roots – was slow to make an impression in East London. The first two punks I ever saw in the locale were at the Lacy Lady, a soul club in Ilford. Dyed and cropped barnets, bin liners, with multiple safety pins in their ears. To confuse matters, they were dancing – and dancing well – to 'Hard Work' by American jazz sax player John Handy. Love a bit of subcultures bumping heads in the dark.

The Spooky Lady, another club over Hackney Wick, had started putting bands on and myself and Dave had gone there to see Geordie band Penetration. The only other punters were two girls who seemed to have got most of their fashion tips from old St Trinian's movies. As an attempted nod to the times, one had written 'SHIT' on her forehead and the other 'FUCK' in black marker pen on her cheek. The band were okay, if not life changing.

We left before the end and didn't say goodnight to Shithead or Fuckface.

We had Small Wonder, of course. A record shop and indy label in Hoe Street, Walthamstow run by a diamond of a geezer, Pete Stennett. A beanie-hatted hippy with Peel-like eclectic musical taste buds, Pete put out a lot of records by excellent new bands, including the Cure, the Angelic Upstarts and the Cravats. But until he signed us, none of them were local.

So what converted me to the cause? That honour would go to the Damned. I'm talking the original line-up with Brian James. I saw them at the Hope & Anchor and they blew me away. Frenetic three-chord mayhem played loud and fast in a small venue to a young crowd going mental. What a night. Even the walls were sweating. By the time they left the stage, I knew this was it. I had to get the band going.

Kev, Dave and I went to see all the good new bands play. And the excitement got to them exactly as it had me. Suddenly we had three quarters of a band again. Kev also knew a guitarist, Dave Monk. And then we were four.

The songwriting pretty much took care of itself. I'd studied loads of songs I liked and worked out a structure to use as a blueprint. A similar technique would serve me well in the future when I moved into TV and then film. I'm a fanboy when all is said and done. And I always try and learn from the best.

Lyrics came fairly easily to me, and with Dave Monk's bottomless brunch of blistering guitar riffs, songs soon began to fall into shape. Our early efforts were quite generically punky, but other influences quickly started to seep in and things got more interesting. Soon melody lines or lyrics, or both, were dictating the course of the songs, rather than guitar. We were improving with every new tune we wrote.

The band needed a name. I went to bed worrying about it and Leyton Buzzards came to me in my sleep. Would you

Adam and Eve it? Sometimes the universe actually does provide. I liked it and so did the others. Buzzards we would be from that day on.

Later every single road sign in East London that included the word Leyton would have Buzzards sprayed beneath it. That always made me smile. My mum was convinced it was me, but hand on heart it was not.

To demonstrate our commitment to the band, Dave and I jacked in our jobs at the shop. A nation of clothes buyers breathed a sigh of relief.

Two weeks after doing this, we realised we had no money. So we had to get part-time work as industrial cleaners in filthy factories. Very glamorous. But we consoled ourselves it would not be for long. We would soon be ready to unveil our baby to the public. Fame and fortune could be just around the corner.

Then again, so could obscurity and destitution, but it's always good to have a positive outlook.

NB. Brendan's dad had run away from Ireland as a child to avoid arrest for smuggling sugar over the border to help support his family. He spent his life here working on the bins and hating the English. He only ever spoke to me via Brendan even after I learned to drink whiskey and knew all the words to 'The Merry Ploughboy'. After he passed away, the family received a letter containing 'conscience money' from a shopkeeper in Ireland who had grassed him up to the Gardaí all those years ago.

Brendan would go on to become artistic director and chief executive of DanceEast and in 2021 was awarded an OBE in the Queen's Birthday Honours for his services to dance.

A GENESIS OF KINDS

After months and months – well, a few weeks, at least – of rehearsing, the Leyton Buzzards had their first-ever gig. A pukka one as it happens, considering our East End riff-raff provenance: Chelsea Art School, arranged for us by our mate Lisa Ferrari, who was a student there. Lisa would later go on to work for Bryan Ferry's designer Antony Price, where her staff discount was always greatly appreciated by my wardrobe.

Our guitarist at this time was a bloke called Dave Monk, who sold tropical fish for a living and was a big heavy metal fan. Though I don't think these two things were connected. Most of our early songs were built around Dave's blistering guitar riffs. We sounded like Motörhead, only fronted by a couple of ponces who enjoyed dressing up and really wanted to be in Mott the Hoople. Dave would eventually get 86'd from the band for refusing to take time off from flogging suntanned guppies to play a gig outside London. His first replacement was Mark Banana Fingers, and his name might give you a clue as to why he never got so far as actually playing a gig with us. With the benefit of hindsight, I think the fact he owned a van and a PA system may have had something to do with his successful audition. The geezer had hands like two bunches of ripe

Fyffes, which is not traditionally considered advantageous for a guitarist.

Our third and final axemeister was Vernon Austin Pearce. Vernon could play hard but also boasted a melodic, lighter touch when needed, and the band improved immeasurably as a result. Despite this, the fact that Vernon would never buy a round would always be held against him by his fellow band members, gifted musicianship counting for little amidst a regularly mumbled chorus of 'you fucking tight cunt'.

Anyway, I digress. Back to the art-school gig. Important things first. I wore a pair of striped Wendy Dagworthy drawstring trousers with a matching blouson shirt. I also wrote a song called 'I Don't Want to Go to Art School' especially for the occasion. It had a singalong chorus and quickly became a crowd favourite.

We didn't have that many tunes, so to pad out our threadbare repertoire we threw in the Velvet's 'White Light/White Heat' and the Pistols' 'Did You No Wrong'. It all seemed to go down splendidly with the pogoing minions.

Near the end of the set, an overexcited young woman jumped up on stage and started taking her kit off. Seeing this, a friend of ours in the crowd, Terry Messenger, decided to join her. I loved Terry. He was funny and clever and completely hapless. The boy had no hap whatsoever. His life was a series of self-generated disasters which quickly morphed into anecdotal gold dust. He was also an Irish Catholic with a strong physical resemblance to Woody Allen. On this occasion that look was enhanced by a torn jacket with a tastefully emblazoned swastika and an open bottle of Hirondelle clutched in his right hand. Not his first of the evening, either. Terry cavorted with the half-naked woman while pouring wine over his own head and snarling at the crowd. He was in his element.

It was a picture of Terry, capturing him perfectly in said element, along with the wine, the woman, the Nazi insignia, and of course the snarling, which would appear on the front page of our local newspaper, the *Walthamstow Guardian* a few days later. Post-Pistols and Grundy, this was not such a big deal you might think. And I wouldn't quibble with that.

Other than the fact that Terry's dad happened to be the Mayor of Walthamstow. So the ensuing furore was not inconsiderable. The paper had a large circulation and overnight we became big in parts of East London and large swathes of Waltham Forest. Shea Stadium was now firmly in our sights. The Buzzards were on their way.

BUZZARD MANSIONS

Buzzard Mansions was a flat at the Bakers Arms, Leyton, above our landlord, Irving Philips, the optician. Bass player David Jaymes and I moved in there in 1976 and it soon became the centre of all band activities, as well as the venue for our weekly poker school.

Buzzard Mansions was a dump when we moved in and a dump while we lived there. Though it had gone downhill considerably by the time we left. It came with gaping, great unattractive holes in the front-room walls. Dave and myself, who spat in the face of DIY, came up with an innovative way of dealing with these. Using wallpaper paste, we stuck sheets of newspaper over the holes and then painted them white to match the walls. This worked on two levels. 1: It actually looked okay. 2: Every now and then a visitor would casually lean against a wall in the wrong spot and fall through.

Outside our front-room window, about eighteen feet above the ground, was a giant pair of spectacles, the crowning glory of Irving the landlord's shop frontage. Having some paint left over from decorating, I celebrated the first night in our new drum by risking life and limb to add a pair of boss eyes to the specs. This did little to endear us to our new landlord: a situation which quickly worsened due to our reluctance to get involved in the paying of rent and such like.

Our upstairs neighbours were Brian and Linda. Brian was a photographer and something of an early metropolitan man. He introduced me to things like wok usage and fresh vegetables, for which I remain grateful. But he was not such a metropolitan man that he wouldn't regularly entertain us by bending over naked and making a bunch of hemorrhoidal arse-grapes pop out his aris on request. Brian had a mate named Colin. Colin was into yoga and meditation, and seriously believed all human beings had the potential to levitate. We seriously believed he was a cunt and encouraged him to give it another go at every available opportunity. Both Brian and Colin were happily married when we moved in. Two years later, when we left, they were divorced. This became known as the Buzzard effect.

As our finances went from dire to totally fucked, we gave up rehearsing at the Allan Gordon Studios and started to have full-on band practice in our front room. Local fans heard about this and would turn up with beer. There were some wild nights, which not surprisingly incurred the wrath of the Old Bill, furious neighbours and, inevitably, Irving the landlord. We had to endure a constant stream of protests and threats at our front door. This annoyed me every bit as much as a punk gig played in a one-bed flat on top of an optician's annoyed them. Again, lateral thinking provided a solution. We changed the locks and removed the doorbell. We were bothered no more.

Eventually we received a legal missive from Irving the landlord saying that unless he was allowed access to his flat, he would be attending the premises on due date with a locksmith. We passed this over to our legal people – a gigantic psycho ex-con fan named Womble, who occasionally did security for us and nicked us our dinners from the local super-market – for his informed opinion. The Right Honourable Womble said 'fuck him', and we concurred. Irving the land-lord showed up with his man and drilled out the locks to our front door. But his triumph was short-lived. As he tried to open the door, it still would not budge. We had nailed it to the frame. From that day on our front door would never again open. You could only get in or out by climbing through the kitchen window.

AN OKIE FROM MUSKOGEE

I have always been rather partial to Merle Haggard's redneck anthem 'Okie from Muskogee'. I particularly like it when he sings the praises of 'manly footwear'. Not just because it makes me laugh – which it does – but it also reminds me of a girl I used to know who really was an Okie (native of Oklahoma) from Muskogee. Her name was Cynthia Manley. Were she to have married a man named Hank Footwear, she'd have become Cynthia Manley-Footwear.

But that's by the by.

I met Cynthia in the early eighties while touring America with my new band Modern Romance. Despite being a full-on country gal and more fun than you could fit in a hillbilly's bucket, Cynthia was the singer on the Boys Town Gang song, 'Cruisin' the Streets' – a graphic paean to casual, male-on-male sexual encounters set to a jaunty disco beat that was hugely popular in US gay clubs at the time. It was also, incidentally, the first song I ever heard that discussed cock size, at, well, any great length.

Our own tune 'Can You Move' was riding high at the top of the *Billboard* Dance Charts, courtesy of a ground-breaking nine-minute remix by DJ Richie Rivera and the gay club crowd that had gone nuts for it. And so it was that the Boys

Town Gang and Modern Romance came to be touring a succession of gay venues across the States together.

I'd been hanging around gay clubs in London since the early seventies. Places like Bangs on Charing Cross Road and Yours Or Mine at the Sombrero in Kensington High Street. These clubs had sprung up in the capital after the Sexual Offences Act 1967 had decriminalised private homosexual acts between men aged over twenty-one. I guess the sense of relief was so palpable the gays all wanted to go out dancing to celebrate. I liked these clubs because they had the coolest music and the best-dressed, most interesting punters. Yours Or Mine had a DJ who spun his tunes from beneath an arch decorated with flowers and boasted a multicoloured raised dance floor that looked like a boxing ring. To conform with the UK's archaic licensing laws, it also set out a pressed-meat buffet on a trellis table. If they served dinner, they could also sell alcohol and play music. It is said that Bowie had visited the club and some of the outfits he saw would later influence his look for Ziggy. I cannot vouch for that. But I do like to think of Bromley's first son throwing a few shapes alongside the disposable plates of Spam and potato salad.

Such quaint establishments were to prove scant preparation for their US counterparts, which we now found ourselves performing in. Clubs like the Glory Hole, the Mineshaft and the Anvil.

Especially the Anvil.

In a previous life it had been a three-storey hotel and bar catering mainly to sailors and male sex workers. Now it was a gay BDSM after-hours sex club, and the most notorious establishment in New York. It made Studio 54 look like a glee club.

Walking in, that first time, the smell of a thousand poppers sent my head reeling. Hardcore gay porn was projected onto one wall; naked men were suspended and chained from another. Suffice to say, when they had a whip-round at the Anvil, it had nothing to do with getting the next round in. There was a back room for anonymous sex, and another for those into golden showers. For those into anonymous sex and being peed on, it was thoughtfully only a short walk between the two. There was a stage on the main floor where performances would range from drag queens to live fisting shows, in which the audience was often encouraged to participate: the phrase 'let's give a big hand to the next act' taking on an entirely new connotation.

This was a world of muscle-bound leather clones, a bewildering smorgasbord of sexual proclivities and drugs. Shed loads of motherfuckin' drugs. Quite how the East London floppy-fringe brigade had ended up performing there was anyone's guess.

Being on tour and in such a hardcore gay environment, Cynthia and I, both being straight, started hanging out at after-show parties. We found we had a lot in common. She had a huge appetite for life and me, both of which I shared. We made quite the couple, did me and Cynth: the white, country-and-western gay-disco diva and the salsa-singing rapper from Hackney with a spivvy pencil moustache.

We were playing clubs around the LA area when we were told that the next night's show had been pulled, leaving us with a much-needed day off. Cynthia suggested she pick me up early and we head off into the desert to check out some watering holes. I thought that sounded a splendid notion.

I may never cut the mustard as a life coach, but leaving the city behind and driving through miles of beautiful, dusty American nothingness in a battered convertible with a girl at the wheel and a bottle of Jack Daniel's in your hand is something I would heartily recommend to young men everywhere. I felt like I was in a movie. One in which the location

71

manager had thoughtfully arranged for a series of isolated, cool-looking bars to pop up at ever-convenient intervals. We would pull over, drink beer, do some tequila shots, play a little pool, and then move on.

To younger readers, I should point out that driving while under the influence was not then the social taboo it is today. This was a much simpler time. One where folk could bugger an underage child or have sex with a corpse and still be guest of honour at the local Rotary Club's annual dinner and dance.

At every dive we pit-stopped, Cynthia was warmly welcomed. She seemed to know all the owners and a motley array of boozers, cruisers and three-time losers. And they knew her. She was a popular gal around this neck of the desert. It occurred to me that I may not have been her first. I consoled myself that I was at least her first salsa-singing rapper from Hackney with a spivvy pencil moustache.

As daylight and sobriety became distant memories, we decided to head for home.

Cruising back beneath the shadow of dusk, I felt like we were the only two people left alive on the planet.

This sadly proved not to be the case as, from nowhere, a cop car was suddenly on our jacksy, sirens wailing.

Seriously?

Old Bill of the desert. Who knew?

Cynthia pulled over. It quickly became evident that septic cops were as different as their gay clubs. Guns were flashed and orders harshly barked. They apparently had reason to believe that she was driving while drunk. The three-quarters-empty bottle of Jack sitting in her lap being something of a clue in this exemplary piece of detective work.

At this point they didn't have Breathalysers in the US, instead relying upon a series of sobriety tests. First off, she had to stretch out an arm with her eyes closed, then bring her hand in and touch the tip of her nose. Yup, this was some seriously scientific shit. Cynthia coasted it. I threw her a smile, which she hung on to for good luck.

Next, they asked her to recite the alphabet backwards. Jesus. I couldn't do that now, stone-cold sober. But again, she cracked away, no problem.

Finally, she had to walk a distance of some ten yards in pigeon steps, while maintaining perfect balance. Piece of cake. She tippy-toed along gracefully and crossed the finishing line.

I breathed a sigh of relief.

At which point she spun around, lifted her skirt, curtseyed, lost her balance and fell flat on her deuce and ace.

'You're nicked, love.'

Or the American equivalent thereof.

They searched her motor and found a wrap of coke in the glove compartment. To be honest, I don't think any of us had expected them to find gloves.

They cuffed Cynthia and slung her in the back of the cop car. I protested that I wanted to go with them. The cops responded in the traditional manner when dealing with an uppity, second-tier British pop star in a desert situation by completely ignoring me and driving off.

I was alone. In the middle of nowhere, miles from anywhere and anything.

I thought of phoning my manager to come and rescue me, but then remembered that cell phones hadn't yet been invented. I looked at the car and saw the cops had left the keys in the ignition.

I had never driven in the States and didn't have a US licence. Neither was I insured.

Plus there was the not insignificant matter that I had drunk enough to take down a small buffalo.

I became convinced it was a trap. I'd drive off and the cops would pull out from behind some big fucking dune or whatever and have me bang to rights. I knew I would not do well in jail, being heavily reliant on hair products at that time.

But what option did I have? It was dark, the temperature was dropping, and I could hear the angry squawking of vultures as they began circling above me. Okay, that last bit's not true. But I was bricking it. You get my drift.

So I started the car, switched on the headlights, and pulled away into the blackest of nights.

In truth, I probably never covered much more than a 150 miles, but gripped by fear and with the devil's own hangover now hammering away at my temples, this was the slowest, most painstaking road trip of all time. I sweated every foot of that bitch of a journey. Finally, after about four hours, I reached civilisation. Or as close to it as West Hollywood could ever claim to be.

Day was breaking and there was traffic on the roads. Figuring that a weird-looking drunk bloke wearing a Johnson's antique leather jacket covered in Japanese writing and driving a battered convertible had already pushed his luck to indecent levels, I parked the car and walked the last few miles back to the hotel.

I arrived exhausted and collapsed on the bed fully dressed. As I drifted off towards much-needed sleep, I made a pact with myself to stay away from bad women. The next time I had a day off, I would read a book.

Cynthia didn't fare so well. She was hauled up before a judge who relieved her of her licence and sent her off to a rehabilitation centre. As for me, I saw out the rest of the tour but never did get around to buying that book.

*

NB. A few years back I heard the sad news that Cynthia had died. She was still performing, touring and recording right until the end. I read an online obituary and saw that she had spent time and energy working for AIDS charities in later years. Giving back to the community that had so loved her. She was always a big-hearted girl, and it seems she was a big-hearted woman also. I would say that I hope she rests in peace. But peace was never her thing.

LOST

In the late eighties I brought myself an Aero Highwayman jacket in chrome-tanned horsehide. I'd coveted such an item for a long time. But Aero Highwayman jackets in chrome-tanned horsehide do not come cheap, what with chrome-tanned horses being something of a rarity. Finally there was sufficient spondulix burning a hole in my pocket to make the investment.

Sorted.

Only it wasn't. I thought I'd look like Marlon Brando in *On the Waterfront* in my new Aero Highwayman jacket in chrome-tanned horsehide. In reality I looked more like Boris Karloff in *Frankenstein*. This was the stiffest jacket there ever was. It could stand up independently. If I tried to raise an arm to wave hi to a passing friend, I'd need a lie-down afterwards to recover from the exertion. A few months in, it never came out the wardrobe.

At this point in my story I need to introduce a guest player. My friend, Alexei de Keyser. How to describe the Lexman? He had been a barman at the Groucho in his youth, but when we met, he worked for TV producer Verity Lambert, for whom I was writing a series. Me and Lex hit it off immediately. He was the kind of warm, gregarious, fun-loving bundle of energy for whom words like 'colourful' do scant justice. He had a fondness for the gee-gees and as a result was habitually boracic and owed money all over town. He once told me of the time he was writing out a cheque to his bookmaker – this was back in the day when you still had to write your name and address on the back of a kite – and the 'bastard nag' fell before he'd even got to the postcode. But he'd be roaring with laughter as he relayed the yarn.

The boy also liked his stimulants – be they in liquid, powder or female form. On one occasion, in the wee small hours and finding himself in need of a little pick-me-up, Alexei had stopped off at a pie-and-mash point to draw out the last of his available funds.

Unfortunately, this was on the All Saints Road, where such activities came with a health warning. Money in hand, he turned around to find three unfriendly-looking gentlemen standing before him, one of whom was brandishing a large machete. Before a word was said, Lex pressed the three twenties into the chap's other hand, bade them all a very good evening and walked off. Another day, another anecdote.

Alexei and I saw a lot of each other when I was writing restaurant reviews for *Arena* magazine. He was my regular dinner companion for the simple reason that he loved eating and was huge fun to hang out with. He claimed to be on the 'safari diet'. He had to have 'something that runs, something that flies and something that swims' at every meal. Jeez, could he tuck away the groceries. And for a poor man, his penchant for rich food was legendary. I recall one sitting at the Ivy where he opened with sautéed foie gras on brioche and a glass of Sauternes, moved on to stuffed pheasant with a side of truffled mash washed down with a bottle of heavy red, and then finished with sticky toffee pudding topped with a large dollop of cream and a couple of Armagnacs. After he was done, I literally saw the colour drain away from his face. He turned grey. I walked him for miles that night before a healthier flush returned to his chops.

After eating, Lex and I would continue the evening's festivities at a club. Now I've always been partial to a bit of nightlife, as you may have heard, but the kind of clubs he *schlepped* me to were somewhat removed from my usual haunts. The clientele consisted almost exclusively of *trannies*, as they then called themselves, hookers, gangsters and drunken fools. I liked to think we were there to observe. But, truth be told, we probably drifted into the lattermost category as often as not. One night, in one of these dives, Alexei announced that he'd made the acquaintance of a 'delightful' young working girl and, as a consequence, would like to borrow the sum of £400 from my good self. After getting up from the floor, I explained to him that I was not in the habit of carrying around such princely amounts in my skyrocket. Furthermore, if I had been, sponsoring his proposed set-to with a lady of the night would not be uppermost on my list of potential usages for it. But the Lexman was not for turning. He explained that the barman was an 'old colleague' and was willing to 'take payment' on my credit card and give me the four hundred in readies. Which I would in turn give to the Lexman. He promised faithfully to have the money back to me the next day.

And he was Alexei. And he had this way about him. And to cut a long story short, the deal was struck.

When I phoned the following day, I knew from his 'woe is me' tone that all was not good in the de Keyser hood. Back at Chez Lex, he had paid the young lady in advance, as requested, and then adjourned to the Gary to powder his bugle before battle commenced.

He had returned just in time to see her roar off down the

road on the back of a motorbike. Along with any hope of me getting my four hundred squids back, I thought to myself.

But that same evening Alexei returned to the club and demanded to see the manager.

By all accounts he then tore him a new one. I understand the phrase 'what kind of establishment are you running here?' was used at one point. The manager, while accepting no responsibility for the previous night's shenanigans, actually refunded him £200. Which in turn found its way back to me. Under the circumstances I counted that as a result. I never saw the other couple of ton. But the thought of my affronted friend in an erstwhile brothel complaining about the level of customer service on offer compensated for the loss more than somewhat.

Now I tell you all this for a reason. Alexei loved my Aero Highwayman jacket in chrome-tanned horsehide every bit as much as I had originally. And knowing of the problems I was experiencing with it, he made me an offer. He would take the jacket and he would wear it. Day in and day out, come rain or shine. And when it was nicely worn in and softened up, he would return it to me. Now with the benefit of hindsight I can see a few of the potential flaws in this plan.

But he was Alexei. And he had this way about him. And to cut a long story short, the deal was struck.

The jacket was handed over.

Not long after, I packed in the restaurant reviews, and the Lexman and I didn't see so much of each other. We'd still get together now and then for the odd night of outward boat-pushing. As luck would have it, he never seemed to be wearing the jacket on such occasions. But he was always happy to give me updates and fill me in on its general well-being. It was 'almost there'. Always 'almost there' . . .

Fast forward to 2004. In one of my not infrequent career

swerves, I now fancy myself as a screenwriter and as a result have travelled to the Cannes Film Festival. I'm strolling along the Rue d'Antibes with an independent air, doing a passable impression of Larry Large. My phone rings. It's Abi, a mutual friend of Alexei's and mine. I knew something was wrong the minute she spoke. As I now know, you always do with such calls.

The Lexman had died. Just like that. He had gone and died.

We spoke for a bit, I thanked her for letting me know, and I hung up. Then I fell into a doorway and sobbed my eyes out.

Back home, the great and good turned out in in their droves at Golders Green Crematorium to see this lovely and most vibrant of men off. He was thirty-six years old. That he had packed a lot of living into those thirty-six years proved no consolation whatsoever.

Afterwards there was a bit of a do at the Groucho Club, where I met Alexei's actor father, David. This was disconcerting for me. Not just because he was my dead mate's dad, but also because I already knew him from *The House of Eliott*, a TV show about two posh sisters who ran an haute-couture fashion business in the 1920s, which I had been hopelessly addicted to. *The House of Eliott* was cheese of an order so high it should have been shot in Neal's Yard Dairy. Picture this. With only a week to go before the girls' new collection is due on the catwalk, Evie, the design half of the team and well-fit, younger sibling with a sexual penchant for penniless bohemian artist types, finds herself entirely bereft of inspiration. To relieve the monumental pressure on her prototype feminist yet simultaneously delicate female shoulders, she goes for a stroll around a nearby museum or art gallery where quite out of the blue she sees an outfit from the past that gets her creative juices flowing. She rushes back to work, flush with excitement, stopping only briefly to shag another penniless bohemian artist en route, and shares her bold and fabulous new ideas with Bea, the more business-like and rather prim elder sister, whom we always suspected was really a lesbian.

Within minutes their sweatshop, full of working-class seamstresses with unconvincing cockney accents and unwanted pregnancies, is a hive of industry. The girls all happily grafting until their fingers bleed to get the collection ready for the big day. None of them ever thinking to say, 'Oy, Evie, you've knocked off this toga idea from the ancient Greeks,' because they are working class and have no concept of fashion piracy, or indeed Greece.

Alexei's dad played a kindly business partner who would warn the girls they were on the verge on bankruptcy at the beginning of the first act, and then later bring the welcome news that London's hoi polloi had gone mental for their new clobber and the business had been saved. Until next week's episode at least.

But now I was talking to David, the man who had lost his son, and I was struggling. I'd experienced friends who had lost their parents, of course. And some their partners. But to lose a child? There is no balm to soothe, no words capable of offering comfort. If there's a more wretched hand to be dealt, it is one I do not wish to contemplate. Perhaps sensing my discomfort, Alexei's dad asked me about the restaurant reviews. I began telling him about some of our adventures. But then part of my brain would race ahead and send back a warning of some impending adult content which it would not be appropriate to share with the recently departed's father. The stories fizzled out. Threadbare yarns in search of a punchline.

As we chatted, I remembered my Aero Highwayman jacket in chrome-tanned horsehide. And I'm a little ashamed to admit that I wanted it back. I mean, it was mine. And it had cost me many pretty pennies. But now it would also be a keepsake of my dear friend.

I said nothing, of course. And I've never seen the jacket again to this day. I hope it found a good home and that its current owner knows something of its provenance and the life force it had once contained.

I recently saw one pictured on a website and it all came flooding back. I realised that in truth I hadn't missed the jacket at all.

But my good friend Alexei de Keyser? Well, that's a different story altogether.

MOTHER AND DAUGHTER

My daughter Nell and I sat with my mum in the hospital. She looked grey of pallor and so terribly frail but was somehow in decent spirits. We tried feeding her some lunch, but she wasn't interested. Knowing her eating habits of old, I produced some crisps and dark chocolate and she smiled and ate a little. Sugar and salt: 1 – Healthy eating: 0. As I looked at her lying there, I could see history, a thousand memories, and my own connection with my past. The old East End, soup kitchens, fascist marches, the war, evacuation, the council flats I would clip-clop home to in my first pair of Blakey-pimped wing-tips. And my late father. His proud face as he arrived home in our first car, our family holiday abroad to Rimini, the day he drove to my gig in Cornwall to tell me my granddad had died. I am scared of the things I won't remember when mum isn't around any more. History is all bold, broad strokes, with small things forgotten, detail lost. And life lives in the detail. Right now that detail feels so very important. Cynthia in the next bed was having a bad day. She kept yelling that she could 'smell the evil'. Maybe it was the microwaved lunches. Either way, Cynth wasn't having it, and at one point she angrily swept her food and drink crashing to the floor. It was a burst of life I quite welcomed. She then hurled a stream of insults and abuse at the nice couple opposite, who were quietly talking to an elderly relative. They stared at their feet awkwardly, the way people do when they're accused of being in league with the devil during a hospital visit. Then a figure appeared in the doorway. A man in his seventies, wearing PJs and a belted silk dressing gown. His hair was greased back and he sported heavy-framed glasses. Despite missing a few Hampsteads, he looked undeniably dapper. What I noticed most was the big smile on his face.

'Hello ladies,' he announced loudly to one and all. 'I am in bed number nineteen.' He didn't say, 'if anyone's interested' but he didn't have to. As the nurses rushed to throw him out, Nell and I pissed ourselves laughing.

A few minutes later, outside in the corridor we held each other and cried together. It was that kind of day. I see a lot of my mum in my daughter, and cuddling her, feeling her young, healthy life in my arms made me feel better. It was the past and it was the future. With me stuck in the middle, for now at least.

ANIMAL CRACKERS

After my wife and I split, we entered into a shared parenting arrangement for our three young children, Woody, Nelly and Otis. I suppose that's the best you can do in a bad situation, but I hated it. Hated my family being broken up, hated the perpetual impermanence, knowing that in a day or two I would have to say goodbye all over again. The saddest thing I have ever seen is a child's empty bedroom.

Once, when Otis, my youngest, was staying with me, we looked after a rescue dog for my friend Jeremiah while he was away on holiday. He was half chihuahua, half Jack Russell. That's the dog, not Jeremiah. Jeremiah's a brick-layer, brilliant self-taught physio and superb swimmer who gives silent lessons to autistic children at a local pool. He's also, by the by, a lifelong Stranglers fan, a former West Ham hooligan and once shagged Siobhan from Bananarama. With a CV like that, it's probably him that should be writing a book, not me.

The dog was a puppy, named Tyson. Otis adored him and was sad to see him go. With our first broken-home Xmas on the horizon, I decided to get him a similar cross-bred dog for his present. A little excessive for a four-year-old, but understandable given the circumstances. I thought having a pet at my place would make it feel more like home.

In truth, I'd never been much of a pet person. Animals had not been allowed in the flats I grew up in, so I'd never spent any time around them. There had been an Irish family in the next block whose dad once came home drunk with a horse, but the council made him get rid of it. What with their flat only being a two bed and all. As far as I was concerned, animals were for eating, wearing and betting on.

When I first met my ex-to-be, she bought a shih-tzu, and when she moved in with me, she brought the annoying little hairball with her. My ex was a model and often away on shoots, which meant I had the joy of looking after it. The dog was miniscule and girly-looking. I am a heavily set bloke who's, well, blokey-looking. We looked ridiculous together. When I took it for walks, passers-by would smile in a way that said, 'look at the state of that big geezer with the little gay dog'.

To make matters worse, it absolutely refused to shit outdoors. You could walk it for miles and nothing. But pop into the dry cleaner's to pick up your strides, and *BANG*, the trapdoor would open. 'I'm sorry, I'm so sorry,' I would stutter to whoever had been the unwilling recipient of his latest faecal calling card.

Which, when you think about it, is ludicrous. A grown man apologising on behalf of a dog's anus.

The flat we were living in at the time had a mixer on the bath taps which only worked when it was in the mood, which was not often. So, to run a bath you first had to fill it with hot water, then turn it off and add the cold.

I was sitting reading while the bath was running one evening when the silence was shattered by what sounded like the unearthly howl of a highly aggravated banshee. I got up to investigate and realised it was coming from the bathroom. When I entered, I saw that the hairball had jumped into the bath, which was about six inches full of scalding water. He would leap, screaming, high into the air with his four legs rigid and then land back down in the water, which would cause him to jump up again and so on, and so on. It looked like something from a Tom and Jerry cartoon. I had never seen anyone, or anything bounce up and down in great pain before. Springing into action, I caught him on the volley and rushed him to a vet. Fortunately, no permanent damage had been done. But for months after, his poor, little Scotch pegs looked like an order of Korean barbecue wings.

I was deemed not responsible enough to look after him, which I thought a little harsh. If it wasn't for my timely inter-vention, he might still be bouncing up and down today. But the dog was given away to a friend. A fate that would account for more than a few Deane family pets in the years to come. Not all were so fortunate. When Woody was little, he had a hamster named Stuey. I came down one morning and found poor Stuey brown bread in his cage. I was always telling him to slow down on that wheel of his, but he never listened. Woody was heartbroken. We held a funeral in the garden and my son said a few words. 'You haven't been in our lives very long, Stuey. But you brought us all a lot of joy.' I had a tear in my eye as I shovelled earth over the cotton-wool-lined shoebox that would be his final resting place. RIP Stuey.

Next, we had a cat named Sonny, whom the kids liked, but I thought had a shifty way about him and never trusted. After a while he started spending some time with Pat, a widow from down the road. We saw less and less of him until one day he stopped coming back to our gaff altogether. Dumped by a cat for an old widow. Fuck you, Sonny.

For a time, we had a spirited little terrier called Buddy.

We also had a miserable neighbour called Mr Tobe, whom the kids promptly rechristened Mr Toad. After a while he was simply known as Toad. Toad was the kind of grumpy curmudgeon who would call the police if the kids were skateboarding on the front or riding their bikes on the pavement. One day, when Buddy got a little yappy in his general vicinity, he swung a boot at him. It didn't connect, but the incident clearly made an impression on the dog. The following day Toad was getting into his car when Buddy legged it out the house and sank his Hampsteads deep into the man's leg. Now he really did have something to be fucking grumpy about. He went completely radio rental and started shouting the odds about having Buddy put down. I had no doubt his threats were serious, so we had to act quickly. Buddy was smuggled out of the house that same night. Luckily, I knew some people and had fixed him up with a moody passport and new identity. He now resides in Buenos Aires, and the last I heard was running a successful import–export business.

After that we had a snake called Dave, whom I got on okay with. Dave was my kind of pet. He'd chill in his vivarium and didn't require much attention. You had to feed him dead baby mice, which is no one's idea of a day at the seaside, but that aside, he was no trouble. Until he started to grow. He got stronger and smarter and eventually figured out how to open the sliding door to his snake crib. At which point he would have it away on his toes. Not literally of course, as he didn't have any. The shout would go up – 'Dave's out!' – and the family would run around like blue-arsed flies trying to find and recapture him. He was the Ronnie Biggs of the reptile world. His favourite hiding place was a drawer in my library directly beneath my collection of Alan Bennett books. Which is quite sophisticated taste for an animal whose main aim in life is usually not to end up a handbag.

One of the things I liked about Dave was that, being a snake, he was always good for a laugh when people visited the house. The kids had a maths tutor who'd come over once a week. His name was Tony, and he was a huge African fellow with a commanding presence and a tendency to crowbar God and Jesus into every conversation. The word overbearing was designed to describe men like Tony. Quite how my daughter Nell worked out he was terrified of snakes I do not know. But the sight of a nine-year-old girl holding one and chasing a screaming, six-foot-five geezer around the house remains amongst my most treasured pet memories.

Eventually the day came that Dave busted out, and try as we might, we could not find him. We turned the house upside-down, but he was nowhere to be seen. Dave had gone. No tears were shed because, well, at the end of the day, he was a snake. But there was genuine concern about his well-being. How would a domesticated snake survive in the wilds of South Woodford?

I'd read there were snakes in Epping Forest. I told the kids that he'd no doubt find his way there and soon make new friends. After all, it was only six stops away on the Central line.

The following year the dishwasher went on the blink, and I called in a bloke to repair it. I explained the problem and left him struggling to manoeuvre it out of the unit it was housed in. Suddenly a cry of 'fucking 'ell's bells' filled the air, followed by the crash of a weighty household appliance hitting expensive Italian floor tiling. The repair man had lifted the front of the machine and our old mate Dave had slithered out from beneath it. By this time, he was a couple of foot long and had given the poor man quite a start. I suppose it would, really. We all marvelled at Dave's powers of survival. I guessed he had found a leaking pipe to provide himself with water. What he had been eating is something I don't like to think about.

For a period, Dave resumed his status as family pet. That didn't last long, due to his stubborn insistence on continuing to grow. The bigger he got, the more like a real snake he became. The baby mice he had once snacked on had now been replaced by the fully grown variety. Feeding times were a bit of a horror show and none of the kids would go near him. In the end, Dave went the way of many of his predecessors and was passed onto friends, this time with a son who wanted a pet snake. We were happy to oblige.

But the story does not end there. Within a few months he had done a bunk once again, and no one has seen hide nor hair of him since.

Maybe he did find his way to Epping Forest. Or maybe he's shacked up with Buddy, living it large in Argentina. Who can say? Dave craved his liberty and eventually he got it. Whenever I hear Mick Jones sing 'Stay Free', I think of him.

After all this, I was now getting back in the pet game once again. My history as a man who steadfastly refuses to learn from his mistakes remained firmly intact. I searched online and found a breeder with a new litter of 'Jackachees', as he called them, for sale. I phoned him and arranged to go over.

At this point I had a sudden, if rare, turn of maturity and spoke to my ex. I told her what I planned to do but suggested it would be a nice move for her to come with me to choose it, and for us to give Otis the puppy together. She thanked me for asking and agreed.

Which is how, that following Sunday, we found ourselves in a council flat in deepest Harlow which reeked of weed at eleven in the morning. Seven puppies were running around, and they all looked happy enough. Probably because they were stoned out of their tiny minds.

One of them was the sweetest little thing. He had brown-and-white markings, big eyes and was clearly the runt of the litter. He reminded us of Gizmo from the movie *Gremlins*. Six hundred in readies was handed over to the man with the bloodshot eyes and Gizmo, as he would always be known, was ours. Unbeknown to me, the ex then returned to the council flat in Harlow that stank of week the following day and purchased one of his brothers, who would henceforth be known as Dodger. On Xmas Day that year, my son received two newly born Jackachee puppies, one from each parent. Or to put it another way, twelve-hundred-quid's worth of stoner-reared mutt.

I'm sure there's a book to be written on the antics of competitive, divorced parents. Come to think of it, there's probably two.

Gizmo quickly became a fixture of our family in a way that previous pets had not. His undeniable cuteness helped, but I suspect the different circumstances were the main reason. None of us was looking for any more change. Which was fortunate for Gizmo because, despite his friendly nature, it soon became apparent that he, like most pets, was a monumental pain in the ass. If a fly entered the room, he barked. If he chased it around the room, he barked some more. When it left the room, he'd segue into a celebratory bark. If we had people over, he'd launch into a full-on barking frenzy, running around like a maniac, jumping up at everyone. Not in a nasty way. He was just super-excited and wanted to join in. And beyond barking and jumping around, there wasn't much else in his repertoire, because, well, he's a dog. It's just unfortunate that his limited skill set rendered him such a nuisance. Gizmo was also a sex fiend. He would hump anything. Human, animal, vegetable or, even on occasions, mineral. If there was a canine #MeToo movement, he would be in some serious shit. To make matters worse, although a small dog, he was hung like Ron Jeremy, his excited bulbous lipstick dragging down low across the kitchen floor. It was not a pleasant sight. I decided to get him neutered. The vet said it would calm him down generally, so it looked like a win–win. But as I sat there with him in the waiting room, I began to feel guilty. I remembered the old joke about the townie visiting the country who sees an old farmer about to castrate a bull. He's sitting on a stool with a brick in each hand, one on either side of the bull's testicles, readying himself to smash them together. 'Jesus,' says the townie, 'doesn't that hurt?' 'Only if oi catches me finger,' replies the farmer.

As it turned out, the only pain felt was by me as another 350 quid was handed over for the procedure.

Gizmo recovered quickly, but the promised results were disappointing. He was as excitable and jumpy as ever. I guess I would be too if someone had recently lopped my bollocks off. As for the humping, it carries on regardless to this day.

A few years back, I was seeing a woman, and we returned to the house after an evening out. For once, none of the kids were around and, caught up in a moment of passion, we went at it in the kitchen. I was deep in the zone when I became aware of some movement to my left. I kept going but turned to look. Adjacent to me, a few feet away, was Gizmo. He'd flipped his bed over and was rogering the bejesus out of it. And here's the thing. He was going at it in perfect sync with me. He looked over. I swear if he could have winked and given me a thumbs-up, he would have. My ardour went softer and that was the end of that.

Despite all this, Gizmo slowly inveigled himself into my routine.

Our walks over Wanstead Park and Hollow Ponds are something I've come to really enjoy. Though these days I tend to swerve Hollow Ponds due to its popularity as a dogging and cruising spot.

The last time I had walked the dog there, it was after a spell of rain. We hit a muddy patch and turned off onto a path that led through some bushes. A short way in, we were confronted by a man standing there with his trousers and pants around his ankles while another man was on his knees fellating him. Not what I needed first thing of a Sunday morning. Even Gizmo looked disgusted. Turning back meant negotiating the muddy patch and I was wearing a nice pair of off-white suede Klemans. If you know me and my relationship with footwear, you'll understand that was never going to happen. So, me and Giz kept our heads discreetly down and advanced. Now the path was narrow and the – what's the word I'm looking for? – suckee was stood half on it, with the result that I had to squeeze past him. Our shoulders brushed and I found myself politely muttering 'excuse me, please'.

Why did I say that? I was out walking my dog. He was the one getting his cock sucked 200 feet from the tea hut. Sometimes I could curse my late mother's ritualistic insistence on good grammar and manners.

These days my relationship with Gizmo has taken on another dimension. He's been with us for seventeen years and the fact is, we've grown old together. He's now prone to a spot of arthritis in one of his hind legs and his eyesight isn't what it used to be. The days of him running like a hare through the fields are long gone. Once or twice on walks over Wanstead Park recently he has got lost. Something that has never happened before.

Possibly down to his eyesight, or maybe his faculties just aren't what they were. Something we all know a little about as we age. I injured my knee exercising indoors during lock-down, and two years later it's just starting to dawn on me that

I'm now of that age when it will never be right again. So Giz and I are as two old campaigners treading the fields together. Neither walking too fast for the other to manage.

Nelly now lives with her best friend Bills in my old stomping ground, Bethnal Green. The Woodman has settled in Lisbon. Otis, who is twenty-two, still lives with me. We get on famously, but naturally as he gets older, we do less and less together. He knows his old man's pretty cool, but who amongst us can compete with the charms of the latest blue-haired vegan to have caught our offspring's eye? It's the way of the world, the wheel inexorably turning.

But to this day whenever I say, 'Fancy walking the mutt?' he will always say yes. It is unsaid, but my guess is he knows this time is important and to be cherished, every bit as much as I do.

OT will not be at home for ever. After that it will be just Gizmo and me. And while I don't care to think about it, seventeen is already a decent innings for a dog. I have never had the remotest interest in remarrying, and both my parents have passed. So, at some point on the not-too-distant horizon, I will be confronted with the prospect of living alone for the first time in a very long time. Fuck that. I'm getting a pet.

CANNES THE CANNES

My film *It's a Boy Girl Thing* is being screened at the Cannes Film Festival. Not as part of the festival, I hasten to add. A high-school body-swap movie replete with a king's ransom of knob gags was never going to be a serious contender for the Palme d'Or.

One of the film's executive producers, Sir Elton John, has also very generously offered to host a party and screening for the film at his chateau in Nice. All in all, I decide an EasyJet return is a solid investment.

I'd been to the festival a few times before and have always liked the South of France.

I once had a six-week stint there with my son Woody when my mum was in hospital in Cannes, recovering from an operation. We'd been on a cruise when she fell and broke her hip. You know a holiday's going well when you see an eighty-year-old Jewish lady leaving the ship in a winch.

This time, in Cannes, I share a flat with David Quantick. David is a comedy writer who won an Emmy for his work on the US political sitcom *Veep*. I only mention that because he has a team of lawyers working around the clock to ensure that you do so every time his name is used anywhere, ever, until the end of time. He even signs his kids' birthday cards, 'from your loving dad, Emmy-Award winning comedy writer, David Quantick'.

The flat is centrally located and decorated nicely. So much so we can even invite people over for drinks. I mean, we don't, but we could have.

There are a couple of snags with the place. The shower cubicle is tiny. And neither Dave nor myself are small people. Also, the exposed pipes and fittings get boiling hot when it's in use. The upshot of this is every time one of us is in the shower, it's a countdown until there's a howl of angry expletives as bare flesh meets scorching metal. This is hilarious for the other one, less so for the naked, wet burns victim.

Then there are the beds. Both have really crappy mattresses which offer about as much support as Jeremy Corbyn at a Maccabi Tel Aviv FC home game. Dave suffers a bit with his Jim and Jack anyway. And so it was on the second day that he gets up and enters our attractive kitchen-diner, bent over at right angles. He is in great pain and cannot straighten up. Dave would remain in this position for the rest of the trip.

Cannes during the festival is host to the great and the good, the rich and the famous, the beautiful and the even more so. But let me tell you, nothing attracts attention quite like two big middle-aged English geezers walking down La Croisette, one of whom is folded over with his jacksy sticking out.

We go into a pharmacy to get something to help with the pain. Neither of us speak French. Everyone stares as Dave struggles to explain, rather unnecessarily given the circumstances, what the problem is. I help out by repeatedly pointing to his protruding rear-end and asking loudly if they have any arsehole ointment. Dave tells me to fuck off.

The first screening at a cinema in the centre of town seems to go okay. I tell Dave that I hate sitting there watching my own work. He says don't worry, so does everyone else. But it gets some good laughs and I'm relieved.

The next day I get a taxi over to the chateau. It had been built in the 1920s as an artist's colony and is the most beautiful home I have ever been in. I'm there early with the film's producer, Steve Hamilton Shaw, Elton and David Furnish. Steve suffers from nuclear-grade insomnia and tells me about his recent stay at a sleep clinic in Sweden in search of a cure. I tell him he should have tried sitting in on a note-giving session with himself and saved his money. We take a stroll around the place looking at the art on show. Lichtenstein, Warhol, Schnabel . . . I could go on. Well, I could if I knew more about art.

I make a decision not to drink for the day. Now I enjoy a drink, sometimes many, but this can, on occasion, lead to difficulties. Particularly if I'm stressed or overexcited. At the *Kinky Boots* premiere a few months previously, I had not been on best behaviour and a prominent Disney exec had told me publicly I would never work in this town again. Yikes. Smitten down by a cliché in the prime of my career. A part of me is now thinking 'fuck you, I'm at Elton's gaff just about to have my film shown' but my rarely seen sensible side decides to err on the side of caution. Elton and David have only ever been nice and supportive, and I don't want to repay that by acting like a dick. So teetotal it is.

The party is great. I meet Liz Hurley, who is super-friendly and as fit as, well, Liz Hurley. I am introduced to Lulu and tell her she really makes me want to shout. Don't get a laugh.

I also get to see Elton transform from a bloke hanging around the house in a tracky to professional Elton – looking sharp, being charming and funny all night long to the never-ending succession of people who wanted to meet and have their pictures taken with him. How do you do that? He was awesome.

I successfully swerve the river of pink champagne being diverted our way by a team of waiters who look more like Greek gods than regular serving staff. But there is still a disaster of sorts. Which is not down to me, I might add.

The whole point of the evening is the screening and promotion of the film. Only the film never turned up. It had been couriered over by the distributor in London. It transpires that when such international packages hit their destination country, they are auctioned off to local couriers for the final, to-the-door delivery. Ours had been picked up by a small father-and-son firm who, as luck would have it, didn't work Sundays. And there was no way to get hold of them.

So, as we all gathered at this lavish bash to watch my film, my film was sitting in a lock-up down the road, owned by Jacques Bonhomme and his first-born, Nobby. You couldn't make it up.

But I was still buzzing. It had been a night to remember.

In fact, I continued to buzz all the way home the following day. Right up until the moment I open my front door to discover a pipe had burst and water was pissing out all over my ground floor. At two in the morning, I am still ankle deep in it, on the dog and bone to an emergency plumber, trying to work out what the fuck a stopcock is. It is of juxtapositions such as this that the fabric of my life is so divinely tailored.

MOTHERS AND SONS

Recently I took the 86-year-old mother – think a senile Don Corleone with a Zimmer frame, only dressed as Tootsie – to Specsavers.

'My mother has an appointment.'

'For an eye test?'

'No, for a hip replacement.'

The assistant stares, almost blankly but not quite. Like a thought has just cut through a barbed-wire fence in her head and is slowly crawling along on its belly into the bit of her brain that deals with talking and shit. 'Is that a joke?' she hazards.

'Yes, but it's okay. I don't think anyone noticed.' Mum is led off.

'Don't worry,' she says, 'I'll be back as soon as this damn war is over. I've packed plenty of blankets.'

I wish her luck as I wave her goodbye.

After, we meet my ex-wife and the kids in Costa. My mum wipes out a toasted bacon and brie panini in a matter of seconds. She looks all wrong in Costa. Wrong with her panini. Like a gladiator in the Apple Store. But she enjoys her outing.

Sipping on her almost-bucket of cappuccino, Mum, at one point, tells my ex-wife that she was reminded of the need for an eye test when she saw me wearing my Specsavers baseball cap.

Now I'm pretty sure Specsavers have never made promotional baseball caps. And if they had, I'd have been more likely to set fire to one than wear it. But none of that matters.

I am now the butt of a joke which will run, more or less, until one of us dies.

Oh well, I think to myself, *at least it never came out during the divorce.*

SATURDAY NIGHT'S ALRIGHT FOR FIGHTING

The wild-eyed man in blue is spitting hellfire and shouting the odds. With his shaved head and bag-of-walnuts physique accentuated by a hideous spray-on t-shirt, he looks like Ross Kemp after someone's nicked his lunchtime baguette. He clearly wants a tear-up. The object of his rage, a slim man wearing sunglasses and bad jeans, equally clearly does not. With so many people watching, he can't back down, but his shades cannot hide the fear in his eyes. He tries to walk the tightrope between standing his ground and inwardly praying to God to please make it stop. Never works, that. Walnuts closes in on his prey, ready to go to war.

What's it all about? Who knows? It is possible that the two men are co-directors of a thriving tech start-up and a forensic audit has revealed that Shades has been siphoning off company funds into his private Swiss bank account. But I think that unlikely. This seems more your common-or-garden 'you spilt my pint' kind of conflict.

All nonsense, of course. What's really going on is Walnuts is playing to the gallery, showcasing his alpha credentials to the crowd. Strutting around like a lobotomised Maximus

Decimus Meridius. If needs be, he will reinforce his status with his nut, a fist or a boot. The crunch of bone, a shock of claret to fill the gaping void in his manhood. It's so much easier when idiot blokes are rich. They buy stupid, flashy sports cars, their penis doubles in length and that's that. Sadly for Shades, there is no Ferrari parked in Walnuts' driveway.

Just as it's about to kick off, a short black fella puts himself between the two men and looks Walnuts dead in the eye. 'Take a breath, mate,' he says calmly. That's it. No threats, no showboating. If you've been exposed to the odd bit of rough and tumblage over the years, you get an instinct for what's what in such matters. *He's the one I'd be wary of*, I think to myself. While standing close to a foot shorter than Walnuts, he is himself solidly constructed, albeit with a little excess Pilsner padding around the middle. But he is all quiet confidence.

He wears it like a well-written backstory. If push comes to shove, he knows he's got this. And at that moment so does the unit standing before him. The dynamics shift. Now Walnuts has to back down without losing face. It's all over bar the shouting, which he still does a fair bit of, only from a safe distance while walking away. The show is over, the crowd starts to disperse, and I sit there thinking how good it is to have the pubs open again after lockdown.

WOTCHA, MATES

The year is 1982. Modern Romance has been asked to play at a Warner Brothers conference to be held at a country estate owned by drag artist Danny LaRue. Which is not a sentence one bumps into often. The band has just had its first couple of hits and is flavour of the week at Warner's. The conference is an excuse for record-company people to get together and congratulate each other on the success of the music you have made. Are you following this?

None of us is much inclined towards being house band at a suits' ball. But Brian, our manager, insists we would be helping our careers. Brian is a pub landlord from Manchester who once managed someone or something called Leif Garrett. Naturally, we take his advice.

I should flag at this point that our track record in 'helping our careers' historically falls somewhat short of exemplary. On one occasion when we were struggling to break through, Brian had taken David Jaymes and myself to a private club called Morton's, where we were charged with ingratiating ourselves to a Radio 1 DJ named Andy Peebles. Dave and I didn't know who Andy Peebles was, yet alone what ingratiating meant. But from the moment he arrives, one thing is evident. He is – how can I put this delicately? – somewhat porcine in appearance. We are talking roughly a chromosome away from a rasher of smoked middle back. Despite this, we spend the evening sucking up, as per our instructions. Only while running a side bet on who could surreptitiously snort the loudest or most crowbar the word 'oink' into any given conversation.

As ever, the two dapper-suited overgrown schoolboys amuse themselves no end. As ever, we do not make the Radio 1 playlist. Should Andy ever read this, I can only apologise for our immature behaviour that night. You really should have turned (your curly little pink) tail and walked away.

We arrive at Walton Hall in Warwickshire and Danny is nowhere to be seen. I don't know why I thought he'd be there, but I'm disappointed. I'd wanted to meet him. My parents had taken me to see him perform when I was young, which was my first experience of drag. As a kid I didn't really know what to make of it all. He was dressed as a very glamorous woman but was clearly a man. He sang songs like 'I'm Just a Girl With a Little Bit More' and made some gently risqué gags, but every now and then would switch to an exaggerated Sarf London accent and shout out 'Wotcha, mates!' to the audience, as if to reassure us he was really a bloke. To be honest, I don't think anyone needed reminding. But the audience loved him. In the sixties Danny LaRue was a huge star and household name. Which may not sound that big a deal these days, what with RuPaul, *Kinky Boots* and drag generally coming at you from all angles. But this was an obviously gay man, cross-dressing and camping it up on stage at a time when homosexuality was still very much illegal. And people couldn't get enough of it. What a strange little country we are.

Strolling around Walton Hall, it strikes me Danny has done okay for himself. It's quite a gaff.

We find ourselves sharing a dressing room with Carlene Carter, the stepdaughter of country legend Johnny Cash. I am introduced to the lovely Miss Carter, who mistakes me for a hairdresser. I consider putting her right but instead recommend a combination of tea-tree oil and mint-based products to deal with her troublesome greasy scalp.

There's a lot of hanging around and a free bar. Never a winning combo for us lot. Carlene and her posse take the stage and they're good at what they do. Their brand of old-school country soon has the old-school cunts up on their feet.

This brings out the Deane competitive streak and I'm keen to prove that the East End and Essex hairdressers' ensemble are a match for anything Nashville can throw our way.

Before we go on, I pull the boys in for a morale-boosting huddle and cannot help but notice that John Du Prez, our trumpet player, has breath like a pub carpet.

Just how much has he had to drink?

We bound on stage suited, booted and ready to rumba. Beyond all the fucking about and clothes and shit, we are actually good at this. A tight band of excellent musicians with a crowd-pleasing set. And while my vocal talents peak somewhere short of mediocre, I dress well and am not unduly hampered by confidence issues on stage.

Our opening number is a trumpet-led instrumental entitled 'Who is John Du Prez?'. It has a *Hawaii Five-O* vibe and gives John's lip a serious workout. It opens with bass and drums. As the rhythm kicks in, the suits and suitesses are already starting to move. Oh yes.

They are *ours*, baby.

Du Prez strides meaningfully to my mic at the front of the stage, brings his instrument up to his mouth, blows long and hard . . .

And vomits copiously into his trumpet.

When I say 'into his trumpet', there is only so much puke a trumpet mouthpiece can hold, it not having been designed specifically with such a purpose in mind. The remainder, which is to say most of it, sprays out in a conical trajectory over the people dancing at the front. I really don't have the words to do this debacle justice. Remember that scene in *Carrie* where Sissy Spacek gets crowned prom queen and a bucket of blood is dumped on her head? The shocked reactions of her classmates, exaggerated by slow motion. The sheer disbelief at what they have just witnessed.

Pretty much that. Only with sick and record-company executives. A showbiz trooper like Danny would have been horrified.

Du Prez then turns around and walks calmly off stage. He does not return. I hear later that he throws up some more and then goes to sleep on the floor.

Back on stage, we are left to cope with the aftermath. Not to mention the rest of the set without a trumpet player. And every song revolves around an integral, hooky horn line and solo.

I said earlier that the Modern Romance boys were all top-drawer musicians. I should qualify that. They all were, except for our keyboard player, Robbie, Dave's younger brother. Robbie had been our mate, was great fun and we had always hung out with him. After the band had their first hit, we did not want him to miss out, so had asked him to join the band. He did have the built-in advantage of already looking like a pop star. Unfortunately, he also had the built-in disadvantage of not being able to play any instrument. We bought him a synth, which we taught him to play with one finger, and he would always be buried low in the mix. He promised to learn properly but got so caught up in the business of being a pop star that he never got around to it.

Which was unfortunate, as it turns out, because on this night the only other instrument capable of playing John's parts was Robbie's. Credit to the boy, he did give it a go. But a synth played with one finger by a bloke who up until recently was selling insurance to nurses doesn't sound much like a top-notch trumpet player in full flow. And while Robbie does manage to pick out a lot of the right notes, they are rarely presented in the right order.

It is horrible. An embarrassment. A creeping death in instalments. If I'm forced to describe the feeling I got from the audience that night, I'd be hard pushed not to include words like 'disgust' and 'sheer unadulterated hatred'.

Not brilliant for a pop group. Even less so when the audience are the peeps responsible for flogging your records. .

Like I said, 'helping our careers'? Not a forte.

NB. John Du Prez played lead on our version of Pérez Prado's 'Cherry Pink and Apple Blossom White' – a song I had cribbed from one of my favourite movies, *Diner* – and it reached number 15 in the charts.

After leaving the band, he went on to compose scores for several films including *A Private Function*, *Monty Python's The Meaning of Life* and *A Fish Called Wanda*.

THE ART OF NOSH

Many years ago someone asked me how I'd describe Jewish cuisine. 'Lots,' I replied. And there was some truth in that. I grew up with people who would tuck away the groceries like nobody's business. Big portions consumed at some pace. As though scared a bunch of shashka-wielding, Jew-hating Cossacks on horseback would turn up any second and bring the repast to a premature conclusion.

When my nan died, we found dozens and dozens of tins of food hidden away in her flat. A hungry child has a long memory.

My earliest recollections of joyful eating were my dad arriving home laden with bags from the Brick Lane Beigel Bake. Still-warm beigels and crusty onion platzels with all the fillings. Cream cheese, smoked salmon, chopped herring, egg and onion, chopped liver.

Delicious food that would go down a treat and then 'sit on your chest' as a reminder for the next two days. It was always good to have a tin of Andrews Liver Salts handy on beigel nights.

The Beigel Bake is still there today, and I always make a point of dropping by when in the locale. As do my kids. That pleases me. I hope they'll take their kids there too one day.

It's funny how we're taught to embrace change, yet the places we like the most are often those that have not succumbed to it. Places with some history and tradition. Places that speak of real people, and their place in a community. You don't get that with a franchise roll-out, baby.

The clientele of the Beigel Bake has evolved over the years. Especially in the early hours. Whereas once you'd have seen groups of cabbies huddled together for a snack and a moan about business, these days you're as likely to find a motley selection of students, clubbers and cross-dressers gathered from all over the world. And that is precisely how it should be, of course. Exactly the same but totally different.

London's Jewish delis used to be a feature of the city. Now they are something of an endangered species. As a kid, one of my favourites was Mossy Marks, which was on the corner of Wentworth Street and Toynbee Street in Petticoat Lane Market. Superb smoked salmon and *schmaltz* herring, pickles sold from the barrel, crispy latkes served with a *schmear* of hot mustard in a sheet of greaseproof paper. Just the thought makes my memory water. Petticoat Lane had been a Jewish market since the 1840s and I always loved strolling around there. As well as the great food on offer, it was also my first experience of traders as showmen.

'Cuts and dices, grates and slices, all your fruit and veg,' barked the man behind the stall as he deftly demonstrated the amazing versatility of the contraption he was selling. The same contraption that would be a useless piece of crap by the time you got it home.

My favourites were the crockery salesmen. They would gather up an entire tea service in their arms, throw it high into the air, and catch it all without a piece breaking. Who wouldn't want to drink from a cup that could do that?

When I was ten or so I'd been sent to the Jewish Lads'

Brigade, which was supposedly like a Jewish version of the Scouts but was a bit too quasi-military for my liking. Lots of marching around and polishing belt buckles, all that bollocks. I hated it. I especially hated our lieutenant, a shiny little buttoned-up, red-faced fucker, name of Shad, who bellowed at us like he was personally leading the liberation of Europe. He scared the shit out of me. Well, he did until the day I saw him down the Lane flogging cups and saucers. He saw me laughing and his red face deepened a shade or two. I saluted him and fucked off.

Wherever I'm living – which is always somewhere east – I still check out any Jewish delis in the area. After moving to Woodford, I found a nice little establishment close to Gants Hill, which was known as the Bookshop. I don't know why it was called that as I never once saw a book in the place. But its beigels, platzels and fish balls were top drawer, and I soon became a regular customer. Another advantage of frequenting the Bookshop was Paula, the daughter of the people who owned it, who also worked there. Paula was a delightful girl and also, as luck would have it, a very beautiful one. I figure a lot of the male clientele were there as much for Paula as they were for the fish balls. Although their fish balls are extremely tasty.

My cousin Stephen becomes very taken with Paula and the two of them start dating. I have no problem with this. In fact, I like it. As family, I now sometimes find myself on the receiving end of an extra couple of beigels or a free jar of pickled cucumbers.

All appears to be going well until Cousin Stephen confesses to a few of us that all in the garden of romance is not entirely rosy. As delightful and as beautiful as Paula is, it seems that when he sees her of an evening, her hair sometimes carries with it the aroma of the workplace. I believe both fried fish and pickled herring are mentioned. Everyone Cousin Stephen confides in finds this as funny as he does distressing, and during the course of the conversation someone calls her Paula Platzel, which is a name that very quickly sticks.

Now Stephen has two problems. He does not want a girl-friend whose barnet smells of fish nor one who will now and for ever be known as Paula Platzel.

So he breaks it off.

The next time I pop into the Bookshop there are no more extra beigels and the only free item Paula gives me is the cold shoulder. Now I have to find a new deli. As Cousin Stephen is back on the market, I decide to search out one that only hires unattractive staff to avoid any further changes to my routine.

We never really ate out much back in the day, but now and again the family would go to Bloom's kosher restaurant in Whitechapel. Its walls decorated with monochrome pictures of old East London street scenes, Bloom's was well known for its Ashkenazi (East European Jewish) cuisine. Salt beef, latkes, of course, and borscht – beetroot soup eaten cold with a dollop of smetana (like sour cream, only circumcised). As the years rolled by, it became equally renowned for its octo-genarian waiters. My wife and I were sitting there one night as they were closing up, waiting for a cab we'd ordered that hadn't shown. The old boy that had served us offered to give us a lift home. Remembering how long it had taken him to shuffle to our table from the kitchen and how his shaking hands had deposited half the soup in the tray, we thanked him for his kindness but decided to get a bus.

Bloom's was also known for its practice of leaving food outside at the end of the night for people that were living on the streets. The first restaurant I had ever heard of doing such a thing.

The Whitechapel Bloom's closed its doors for the last time

in 1996. The Jewish community had moved on from the East End and there was by now a myriad of food choices on offer in the capital.

The spot where Bloom's once stood is now a Burger King. You can probably guess what I think of that.

Despite this cultural obsession with eating, my late mum was not much of a cook. Somewhat ahead of her time, she was always a career gal who regarded cooking and housework as a necessary evil to be dealt with as quickly as possible and with minimum effort. If you ever complained about anything, her advice was very simple: 'Piss off and do it yourself.' Go Mum.

Her idea of a casserole was to empty a couple of cans of soup and veg over a cheap cut of meat and bung it in the oven for ten hours before she went to work. Can't tell you what a treat that was. Greens would be boiled alive until reduced to a watery mush. Even as a child I knew food was not meant to taste like that. I once asked Mum why she cooked them for so long and she said that she wanted to have a hot meal ready for my father as soon as he got in from work. Why she didn't know what time that was after all those years of marriage, I couldn't tell you.

My dad's bland palate did not help. I think he may have actually been allergic to flavour. Mum once daringly sprinkled some garlic powder over his steak as it was cooking, and he refused point blank to eat it.

The one dish Mum would take time and trouble over was her chicken soup, the *pièce de résistance* of Jewish mothers everywhere. Steaming bowls of tasty broth flecked with pieces of carrot and onion. And just in case you thought you were getting away with a relatively healthy option for once, there would also be a matzah ball or four. Heavy dumplings that could double as cannonballs for the Israeli military. To this day I cannot smell a pot of chicken stock simmering gently on the stove without thinking of my mum. Sense memory, peeling back the years in an instant.

In the early seventies, when the fam had a few more disposable readies, eating out took a turn for the better. On special occasions we'd head for a restaurant called Isow's, which was on Brewer Street in Soho. Its basement housed the Jack of Clubs nightclub, named after its owner, Jack Isow. In later years the same premises would become Madame Jojo's.

Now I cannot tell you anything about the kind of food they served at Isow's. What I do remember is that people would dress up to go there and everyone looked very glamorous. It also had red-leather chairs, on the back of which were embossed in gold print the names of various celebrities whom I assume had dined there. Unless, that is, the chairs all had names like Danny Kaye, Rod Steiger and Judy Garland. Unlikely, but it was the seventies.

Isow's was my first sighting of dining out as a social experience. Even at a young age the concept fascinated me. It would continue to do so for many years to come.

In the late seventies, when I scored my record deal with Chrysalis, they wanted us to sign the contract at the Roxy Club in Covent Garden, a grimy punk venue we had played at fairly regularly. I was having none of that. I told them I wanted to do it at Mr Chow, a famous Chinese restaurant in Knightsbridge. I'm sure the Clash would have been horrified, but I'd seen pictures of Michael Caine and Twiggy eating there, and that was good enough for me.

As it turned out, Chow's looked very upmarket, but the food was not unlike a bog-standard Chinese. I was very disappointed. What the fuck had Michael and the Wonder Kid been thinking?

An altogether more bemusing experiencing was a lunch with my publisher from Chappell Music at around the same time – we're talking '77 or '78. He was a lovely bloke named Alan Molina who'd had faith in the band from very early on. Alan was quietly spoken and sophisticated. As I came from a background of noisy ruffians, he was an anomaly to me. But an anomaly I liked and was a little fascinated by. When he asked me out to lunch, I accepted, if only to find out what people like him actually ate.

We dined at a gaff called Hiroko, which was close to his office on Bond Street. It was the first Japanese restaurant to open in the UK. As I looked down at my plate of tiny slivers of raw fish positioned deftly alongside exquisitely sculpted pickled vegetables and miniscule bumps of fiery green wasabi, I thought it may as well have been Martian. I was convinced he'd lost the plot. It would take another ten–plus years for Japanese to become one of my favourite foods. These days, of course, it's one more ubiquitous cuisine we take for granted. I have a terrific Japanese takeaway just around the corner from my home in East London. It's staffed entirely by Indians and Koreans. One more reason to love London.

Over the years, as my situation changed for the better, eating out became a regular feature of my life. And I always loved the social side of it all. Right up until the time that I didn't. Okay, that's an exaggeration. I still eat out and I still enjoy it. But the desire to try every new place someone tells me about has long gone. My love of good food remains una-bated, but my favourite meals these days are when the kids or some friends come over and I get busy at my oil–drum jerk pit in the garden. Crispy chicken cooked over fire with its smoky pimento flavours filling the air, homemade coleslaw and rice and peas. Stuff of the gods. Not a Jewish god, admittedly. But I did grow up in a Jamaican neighbourhood and that's how the world spins.

When my children were young, I showed them how to

make a proper omelette, gut a fish, cook a steak, throw a salad dressing together, roast a chicken, knock up a pasta out of what you can find in the fridge. Basic survival skills. I'm pleased to say they all know their way around a kitchen these days and none of them will ever suffer from malnutrition. But hopefully it taught them a little bit more than that.

I've always believed that a passion for food is synonymous with a passion for life. You have to try new things. Sometimes you get it wrong. Sometimes you overindulge. But every new experience is there to be savoured and add a splash of colour to your day. The worst existence I can imagine is one spent on the sidelines, nervous of getting involved.

Having a bad meal occasionally. Failing in life occasionally. Not the end of the world.

A glass of Andrews will always sort you out.

PISS FACTORY

When I was young I used to wet the bed. Nothing unusual about that, you might think. Plenty of kids wet the bed. Not like me, they didn't. I wet the bed with Swiss-precision regularity and great gusto. Every night for years and years and years. For a time, my mum would get me up, change the bedding, wash me down and put me back to bed. I'd then fall back to sleep and promptly piss again. In the end she stopped bothering. God knows how many gallons of urine I dispensed, all told. If it had all come at once it would have washed away East London. Imagine the headlines. 'Whitechapel lost in pee tsunami. Many feared drowned or missing.'

To make matters worse, this was the sixties. The time of the great nylon revolution. Everything was made of this new wonder fabric. Shirts, cars, the occasional village. And, of course, bedding. So not only did I have the joy of static sparks flying up my arse as I slid into bed, I'd also get to wake up sloshing around in great puddles of piss the sheets point blank refused to absorb. If you tried to roll away from it, it would follow you. Stalked by your own urine.

Eventually medical counsel was sought, in the shape of Dr Berger, our chain-smoking Polish GP. She would literally have a fag on the go as she examined you. As a child I did not find the good doctor a comforting presence. With her thick foreign accent and face half-visible through a lingering tobacco fug, she had the charisma of a Bond villain with a bedside manner to match. She terrified me.

With the benefit of hindsight, I suspect Dr Berger was Jewish and, in all likelihood, had arrived on our shores after fleeing the Nazis. But that was all lost on me as I checked the surgery floor for trapdoors leading to a piranha tank.

These days bedwetting would be treated with mild medication. Or perhaps counselling. Were it that simple back then. Berger went to her cupboard and returned with a contraption which did nothing to dispel my fear of the woman. We are talking two large rectangles of gauze mesh attached by leads and wires to a box-shaped device which looked like it had been purloined from the consul of the Tardis. The mesh was to be placed beneath separate sheets on the bed and the machine turned on. When you pissed, the magic would happen. A red light flashed on and off and a loud buzzer would sound. I think it's safe to say no Nobel Prizes were handed out to the design team.

I was already sleeping on nylon. Or Satan's cotton, as I had come to think of it, with its unnatural feel and tendency to make you sweat in the summer, while leaving you to freeze to death in the colder months. Now, as an added bonus, I had wiry strands of gauze piercing my pyjamas and stabbing me in the anus.

Despite the levels of discomfort, I slept like a log. Right through the flashing light and buzzing buzzer as I peed away merrily. Not so my long-suffering parents, who had to get up to turn it off.

I was hugely embarrassed by my bedwetting. Something you'd have thought my loving ma and pa would have been sensitive to. But not so much. I would regularly be sent off to sleepovers with friends and family. Mum worked for a company that made polythene, and she would bring home huge, thick sheets of the stuff to serve as makeshift mattress protectors. Everywhere I went a large sheet of double-ply polythene would surely follow. Just in case I 'had an accident'. Thousands of nights of consecutive pissing stretching the bounds of what constitutes an accident more than somewhat.

When I was at someone else's house I would be scared to go to sleep and would fight it all night long. That never worked. If I didn't nod of until seven in the morning, the piss fairies were always there, ready and waiting.

One day it just stopped happening. After all those years of misery, you'd have thought the date would have been imprinted on my mind. That I still celebrated the anniversary of that blessed day every year. But it wasn't like that. It was just one more chunk of childhood that disappeared when you weren't looking. Along with playing run-outs, creeping out of bed to watch TV through a door left ajar, and my Secret Sam Spy Attaché Case, which fired plastic bullets out of a hole at one end when I pressed the secret button. Whatever did happen to that? It was brilliant. The button was secret so that your intended victim would not suspect what was coming. Like an eight-year-old sidling past with a shifty look and a large attaché case would not otherwise attract your attention.

Either way, my bedwetting days were behind me.

At the end of 1973 I was in Israel working on a kibbutz. In October the country had been caught off guard by the surprise attack of a coalition of Arab states. Everyone of fighting age had been called up, which left the *kibbutzim,* then a staple of Israeli society, shorthanded. The farms and factories had to be manned, often in still dangerous situations.

Volunteers were sought from around the world, and I had signed up. Quite what a Bowie Boy with a dyed barnet, four earrings and no skills whatsoever thought he would bring to the war effort, I'm not really sure. But it was good to show willing.

I was also enticed by the prospect of adventure. Which says much of the stupidity an eighteen-year-old is capable of.

The work was hard, hours were long, and the weather cold. Days off were few and far between. And being stuck by the Golan Heights in an uneasy post-war situation, there wasn't much to do anyway. No clubs or anything, bruv.

A girl I knew from junior-school days had emigrated to Israel with her fam after her dad had died. We had kept in touch as pen pals for a time. They had settled in Rishon LeZion, a city not far from Tel Aviv. It was miles from where I was, and transport was very difficult. But with a few days off in my back pocket, I decided to hitch my way there and pay her a visit.

The journey took all day. I'm not one of life's hitchers. Riding pillion with a maniac then sharing the back of a truck with some goats did little to change that.

It was good to see my friend and her family again. The last time had been when I was a kid. We were all different people now. It was awkward in the way that such things are.

The home-cooked dinner was very welcome, and my plate looked like it had just come out of a dishwasher when I'd finished. On the kibbutz almost every meal revolved around aubergine, which they grew and were plentiful. They did not grow steaks or pies or anything like that. After eating, my friend suggested we went to visit someone she knew who had just got out of the army. I said sure.

The friend was a young man who couldn't have been much older than me. He was in a wheelchair. He'd been discharged, having lost both his legs in combat. I sat there in silence.

Two things quickly became clear. He really liked my friend. And he really fucking hated me. Which he let me know in no uncertain terms. He hated me for being a prick. He hated me for having legs. He hated me for the life I would have, which would be better than his. I didn't say anything. At that moment I hated myself for all those things too.

We didn't talk much on the way back to my friend's house. I then made my excuses and said I needed an early night. I had no trouble getting off to sleep, perhaps because it was a day I couldn't wait to leave behind.

I awoke in the early hours. A nightmare, maybe. Tossing and turning and soaked in sweat.

At least I thought it was sweat. But my arse doesn't sweat. Not that much, anyway. Fuck.

Fuck. Fuck. Fuck. Fuck. Fuck.

Why hadn't I packed a sheet of polythene?

A MAN I DIDN'T KNOW

There's a newsagent around the corner from me that I use pretty regularly. It opens at 5 a.m. every day of the week, which for an insomniac such as me can be very handy. It was run by a friendly bloke with a thick shock of white hair named Kiran. The bloke, not the barnet. I was never sure of Kiran's provenance. He was dark-skinned and sported an accent not a million miles from Harry Enfield's Stavros character. I never asked where he was from originally. If you do that kind of thing in London with everyone you meet, you'll never get anything done.

I popped round to Kiran's shop last week and the shutters were down. Sellotaped to them was a sheet of A4 paper with a picture of Kiran and a few sentences explaining that they were closed because he had died. I felt sad. I hadn't really known the bloke, but I liked him. And his smiling face and 'hello mate' greeting had become a part of my life. A small part, for sure. But it is from all those that the whole is constructed. And you notice the details more as you get older. As, despite my best efforts to the contrary, I surely am.

I went into Kiran's newsagent this morning and a young guy in his twenties was working behind the counter. I told him I was sorry to hear the news and asked him if he was related. He said yes, Kiran had been his dad. Actually, he said Kiran *is* his dad. Which touched me. He told me the old man had had a stroke some six weeks back and while in hospital they discovered he had advanced cancer of the oesophagus. He was due to start chemo this week, but it was not to be. He had just died.

Chirag – the son – then went on to say he was heartbroken but relieved. He had not wanted his dad to go through what he knew lay ahead. But he also wondered if he was being selfish. Was it him that didn't want to go through it? I told him that either way, it's allowed. I had lost my own dad to cancer when I was young, and he had gone the whole nine yards of operations and chemo. For years after I couldn't shake the image of his sick, emaciated frame. It took a long, long time to remember him as the big, healthy-looking geezer he had been. So yes, I agreed. Quick and painless was better.

He then told me he believes his dad will always be there watching over him. I said I think that the people we have loved and lost live on inside us. I told him the story about how I'd always called both my boys 'butch' when they were little. I'd never thought about it and honestly didn't know why. Until one day my mum told me it's what my dad had called me when I was young. We must have talked over such things for twenty minutes. In the end we were both tearful.

I asked him if he was going to keep the shop on. He didn't think so. His uncle, who worked nights, wanted to retire. And since the Co-op had opened opposite, the business had gone to shit. So, another little dynasty, another family business will fade into the ether of unwritten history.

I paid Chirag for my bits and pieces and wished him a long life. He asked me if I was Jewish and I said yes. He then offered his hand and we shook warmly. As I turned to leave, it occurred to me that I still didn't know where he and his family were from. But it didn't matter. End of the day, we were just two Londoners sharing a moment.

SUEDEHEAD ROMANCE

'Hey There Lonely Girl' was a tune they played at the Tottenham Royal late into the evening, which would cue the young man's scramble to find a suitable dance partner. A time-honoured courtship ritual that today has been largely replaced by swiping to the left or right.

Around, 1968/1969, there was a girl I used to see over the Park Lane end at Tottenham every other Saturday. Laura – sheepskin, stone Sta-Prest, short hair, dead pretty. I had a huge crush on her but had never even seen her outside of a football ground. Until that night. When Eddie Holman sang and implored me personally to ask her to dance. She was a vision. Girls were at that time. Mohair dresses with keyhole backs, Holy Cow tights, loafers. Angels who dropped their aitches. I walked over and smiled, and she smiled back. No words were exchanged as I welcomed her easily into my arms. We danced and it was magic. In the movie it will be shot slow-motion.

A few seconds later I felt a tap on the shoulder. I turned around and a fist connected with my chin. Goodnight Vienna and hello Tottenham High Road. I woke up on the cold pavement a few minutes later. I'm guessing Laura had a boyfriend. I tried to get back in, but the bouncer barred my way.

'You ain't coming back in. You were thrown out for fighting,' said the brawny Irish tuxedo.

'I wasn't fighting. Someone hit me,' I argued.

'That's still fighting. You just lost. Now feck off.'

I don't remember ever seeing Laura again. But those few seconds of magic were worth twenty punches on the kisser. Which in some ways is the story of my life.

Thanks for the dance, Laura.

BALLAD OF THE THREE-QUARTER-LENGTH SHEEPY

I'd been talking to my buddy Bruno, who was driving down to meet his fam in Spain. Being an old romantic, he made a quick detour to Lloret de Mar to visit the spot where he first met his missus, Jenny. It reminded me of my own holiday there in 1971. This was my second holiday abroad without my parents. I still cannot believe we were let loose in Europe at such a young age.

My first solo foreign excursion had been to Rimini the previous year. Fifteen years old. What were my parents thinking?

Rimini had been like dropping into heaven. The sun, the food, the girls, the bars, the clubs, the clothes ...

Especially the clothes. Back at home, the suedehead thing was dying out and the movement was splintering off in different directions. I'd recently had a pair of slightly flared trousers made at a Soho boutique called Carvil. Just along from the Squire shop and Village Gate. Used to wear them with a penny-collared CCS shirt and a Fair Isle tank top. But I wasn't convinced. None of it felt quite right.

Sartorially, it was a time of some confusion.

And then in Rimini I saw them. The best pair of shoes in the history of the world.

They were like nothing I'd ever seen before. These shoes didn't just speak to me. They called out and pointed the way to a future I'd never dreamed existed. These were shoes that would change my life. They were a beautiful, almost antique brown leather, but that was neither here nor there. Because they had this huge, bulbous, round toe. Like nothing I'd ever seen.

There was a line of central stitching running up it and a natty side buckle to complete the look. But none of that mattered. It was all about the toe. This was my first experience of fashion that was intentionally wrong and yet, somehow, totally right. They cost me a ridiculous amount of money. Most of what I had for my fortnight away. That didn't matter. They had to be mine. No question.

Back at home, I wasn't even sure what to wear them with. But I wore them anyway. I took a fair amount of flak from the idiots. Never bothered me. What did they know?

A year or so later, a shop in the West End called Toppers started selling Italian shoes like mine. Not as good, obviously. But they caught on quickly with young metropolitan men who cared about such things. Soon everyone was wearing them, and the shoes became known as Toppers.

It's things like that, that made my teenage life worthwhile.

I've read and watched much over the years laughing at the concept of Brits abroad.

What imbeciles we are. How poorly we travel. These are not my recollections.

Where I came from, we were not well educated. Neither were we well read. And we didn't have the internet to trawl the world while sat on our arses. In my lifetime, package holidays abroad were singularly the best thing to ever happen to working-class people. They opened our eyes to new food, new music, new clothes, new culture, new people. Most of us sucked it all up and used it as a base to keep growing. Because that is the human way. We have an instinct for new experiences. A desire to learn and move forward. Today almost every aspect of our lives is cosmopolitan. The coffees we drink, the extra virgin olive oil and balsamic vinegar we delicately dunk our *focaccia* in, the clothes we wear, the music we listen to. For me it all began with those Thomson holidays.

Back to Lloret. I was away with 'my mate Neil' (the one from 'Plastic Palm Trees') and our friend Steve Harvey, who looked remarkably like the American heartthrob pop star David Cassidy. Which I have to tell you was no great disadvantage for a young buck on the Costa Brava in 1971. Steve's standing gag was 'I went out on a foursome last night. Me and three birds.'

In Lloret de Mar he actually did.

My approach with girls was very different. I was more what you'd call a soppy sod.

Under the foreign sunshine, surrounded by beautiful dark-skinned women, my senses hit overload and I fell in love. My first bona fide holiday romance. As it turned out she wasn't Spanish. She was from Toxteth. Liverpool 8. But Margo was cracking-looking with a good tan, so WTF. We were crazy about each other, and I even spent a chunk of my remaining holiday money on a ring for her. We both swore this would be more than just a holiday romance with the kind of earnestness only two sixteen-year-olds could muster. We were in love. And soon the world would know it. Starting with my parents as soon as I arrived home.

I told them I was engaged to a girl from Liverpool, and they managed a 'that's nice' underreaction. They obviously thought I was a dozy fucker but wisely elected to keep that under their collective titfer. Margo's family didn't have a phone, so we wrote to each other. Boy, did we write. I also started putting money away so that I could go up and stay with her. And her mum and dad and eight docker brothers, as I learned in one of her missives. Oh well. All in the name of love. I'm sure they couldn't wait to meet their clog-wearing, Tottenham-supporting Jew of a future son-in-law.

I finally had enough for my return train ticket and a bit of spending money – probably enough to buy a three-bed semi in Toxteth at the time – and I told Mum and Dad I was off for the weekend. This was when my mum made her move. She knew I had long craved a three-quarter-length sheepskin coat – a much-prized item of clothing at the time and way out of my teenage price range. She offered to buy it for me as an early birthday present. But only on condition I didn't go to see Margo.

This was my mum at her most hardcore. She knew me. She knew my weakness for clothes. And she went for the jugular.

How dare she? What kind of person did she think I was?

I took the offer. Bought the coat the following Sunday from the undercover market in Petticoat Lane. Even wore it home. After which the letters died out and our great love story swiftly followed suit. I'd like to tell you I felt guilty every time I wore my new coat, but that wasn't the case. There would be other holiday romances. But a three-quarter-length sheepy was a three-quarter-length sheepy, know what I mean?

FOREVER YOUNG

It is said that with age comes wisdom. Personally, I'd rather be a dumbass and able to get up from the sofa without grunting.

But I'm not old. Not like my parents were old. They were old when they were young.

Their wedding photos look like a retirement party. Shiny suits, stiff, lacquered hair and so much cigarette smoke they had to put on gas masks to find their way to the buffet table. But me, my generation? We're not like that. We're the young people that never got off the roundabout. Even after we felt a little dizzy. Even after the fair closed and left town.

I cannot be old. I wore full make-up when I saw Bowie at the Rainbow. I once had a beer with Joe Strummer.

Okay. Both dead. Bad example. But you know what I mean. We are an essential, vibrant generation. We made sensational pop culture. Music, movies, books, magazines, *et al.* Sensibilities were unflinchingly progressive. Feminism grew and flourished. And where you have out gay pop stars, gay rights will surely follow.

And we're still informed, still clued in. Neither dazzled nor confused by technology and advance. Determined, at all costs, to remain relevant.

And yet there's no denying that things have changed and the clock is now inexorably counting down.

Tick-tock, tick-tock, tick-tock.

Suddenly the NHS seem obsessed with my health. They've never given a hoot about me before. Now every week there's another letter inviting (*warning*) me to have some test or another. The most recent implored me to send them a poo sample. I've been on *Top of the Pops* and attended my own movie premieres.

Now I'm expected to take my faecal matter to the post office. Am I supposed to send it registered?

Do I need Track & Trace?

How much do I estimate the contents are worth?

I look down at the tiny plastic shit-cup. Jesus, what are they testing for? Leprechaun arse cancer?

Physical decline comes both slowly and all of a sudden. Which is a trick only the devil himself could pull off. Hair thins, waistline thickens. Your sex drive, for so long the beating drum to which you proudly marched, is reduced to a syncopated cowbell that frequently drops out of the mix altogether. And then one day, without warning, it happens. That sofa grunt. From this moment on there is no going back. You are now one of the 'grunt when you get up' guys. Your membership card is in the post. If only you could bend down to pick it up.

Your body, which used to effortlessly repel anything you threw at it, now seems to have suffered a complete crisis of confidence. You can injure yourself doing literally anything. I put my back out throwing a snowball. Something any smug six-year-old can manage comfortably. My neck locked while I was reversing the car and I spent the next fortnight looking left. The entire right side of the world was closed to me. I had to stand sideways to talk to people. At dinner my companions would look on in pity as I sat there shovelling food into my cheek. On the plus side it was super-easy to make new friends while using a crowded urinal.

I now have tennis elbow. It takes the likes of Andy Murray years of smashing balls around at 140 mph to get tennis elbow.

I got it from typing.

Try impressing the guys in the locker room with that.

'You should have seen this paragraph. I was really going for it. I'd utilised symbolism, metaphor, even threw in a paradox. I was almost there, and it just went. I'm lucky I wasn't killed.'

Tennis elbow makes simple things such as picking up a cup of tea very painful and difficult. Which is embarrassing. I don't want the kids to see me struggle with something so mundane and elementary, so I do my best to hide the effort it entails on my part. But the shaking cup and spilled contents are a giveaway. They now think I have Parkinson's.

Despite my best efforts, the kids regard me as a relic from a bygone age.

I mean, we're still close. I follow them on Instagram and everything. But they want me to be old. Because being young is their domain. And on occasions I find myself joining in the game. Intentionally acting in the way they imagine I do.

My son Woody enters with a colleague from work.

WOODY: Dad, this is Glenn.

By way of an introductory special offer, Glenn adopts a goony smile and attempts to communicate.

GLENN: All right, mate?
ME: I'm not your mate, Glenn. We've never met
    before. Let's start with Mr. Deane, or sir if you

will, and then slowly work our way up to Geoff.
How does that sound?

Glenn's goonish grin is frozen for posterity. Woody gives
me a look that tells me when I am properly old, incapacitated
and losing my marbles, I will not be living in his spare room.

The ex-wife getting remarried to a younger man added to
my creeping sense of redundancy. All the kids went to the
wedding. I felt left out. So I texted my ex and asked her if I
could be pageboy. She texted back telling me to fuck off. I
believe Americans call that closure.

Fading social visibility is another depressing fact of life.
Especially if you're unmarried and still like to go out. Most
single people are younger and understandably not at all interested in you. If one is sensible, one takes this on the chin,
of course. But there is always potential for embarrassment.
A while back I was waiting for my friend Steve outside the
Owl & Pussycat on Redchurch Street and a beautiful young
woman walked over and struck up a conversation with me.
I felt flattered. When she got around to asking me if I was
seeing anyone, it was all I could do not to leap into the air
and click my heels together.

'Actually, I'm not,' I replied, following up with a casual
smile that was meant to convey suave or cool but, on reflec-
tion, may have made me look like a stroke victim.

'That's great,' she said. 'Only my mum's an artist, and she's
just got divorced, and I think you and her would really hit
it off.'

Okay, I deserved it. But the pain was real, brothers and
sisters. Very real.

Having money can lessen the impact of ageing. Cosmetic
surgery. Personal trainer and nutritionist. High-end East

European prostitutes. I invested in laser surgery on my eyes some years back. There's no point paying for expensive hookers if you can't see them. I'd worn glasses for reading and working for years, but my sight was going downhill faster than a fat man on a skiing holiday. I went for an eye test and was told I now needed three pairs of glasses. For short, middle and long distance. The notion of taking a bag of assorted spectacles with me on a night out and swapping them over every five minutes like some novelty music-hall act was never going to run. Letting someone fire laser beams into my cornea seemed a reasonable enough alternative.

I was given three options for treatment. They could try and correct my short-sightedness, my long-sightedness, or I could go for bully and have one eye done for each. I went for the latter.

The procedure was quick and uncomfortable more than painful. I remember an unpleasant smell, which if I had to describe it was not unlike the smell of lasers burning your eyeballs.

The ophthalmologist told me the procedure had been successful. I could barely see and felt like someone had thrown a fistful of grit into my eyes, so I took his word for it. After a few days that settled down, leaving me with two eyes with entirely different visual abilities. Which was something of a brain fuck. Remember that scene where Father Ted painstakingly attempts to explain to Dougal the difference between small and far away? I felt like my eyes were having the same conversation, over and over. Eventually the brain adapts to your lopsided faculties, and it becomes the new norm. But I still sometimes find myself closing one eye to focus better on certain tasks. For porn it's always left eye open. No one wants to knock one out over a blurred woman standing thirty feet away.

Tempting as it may be, I try not to be critical of today's young. They have enough to contend with. Dancing to the tune of malevolent algorithms telling them what to buy, what to eat, where to go, what to watch, who to listen to, who to like or not like. Trapped inside a swirling vortex of Sam Fender, *Love Island* and mashed avocado.

No wonder their poor, addled brains are no longer capable of grasping any concept which extends beyond a TikTok video.

I'm always being asked whether, given the option, I would rather be spending my formative years now instead of back when I did. Actually that's not entirely true. I've never been asked that. Literally not once. I haven't even heard such a subject discussed. Despite this, I'm going to answer anyway. On the off-chance it should ever crop up in the future.

One obvious factor is there was no Covid when I was young. No being forcibly housebound. No threat of a fine or imprisonment by virtue of daring to socialise. And no lunatics who'd been vaccinated nineteen times cycling alone in the forest wearing a mask. Who, when they see you walking towards them, would holler out '*TWO METRES SAFE SOCIAL DISTANCING*' at the top of their voices. Which, ironically, was the last sound the forest would hear as you quietly beat them to death with a tree stump.

I'm sure there were health concerns back when I was a kid, but none that I can recollect sticking its nose into my life. Our concerns were more immediate. A friend of mine told me a story recently. He grew up in East London in the sixties and seventies as part of a big Irish family. During the summer holidays both of his parents would go out to work, leaving him and his six brothers to look after themselves. Latchkey kids, as they were then known. They were left no money, and as often as not, with no food in the house. So how did they survive? Fortunately, this was a time when milkmen still used to deliver door to door. People would leave notes in empty milk bottles outside the house telling 'the milkie' what to leave the following day. Not as sophisticated as online ordering, but it did have its advantages. My friend and his brothers would trek the local streets at night, half-inching any notes they found and replacing them with ones of their own. Adding on an extra pint of gold top here, a loaf of bread and some butter there. Maybe half a dozen eggs or a hunk of cheese if the mood took. Milkmen were like mobile corner shops in those days. The next morning the motley crew would rise early and follow the milk-cart on its rounds. As deliveries were dropped off, they would stealthily scoop up the extras and head home for a slap-up breakfast. From time to time they would be spotted by the milkie and a chase would ensue. The carts were battery powered and had a top speed of around 10 mph. No match for a gang of hungry kids.

My friend did not tell me this as part of some Pythonesque recollection of how tough he had it growing up. He was dewy-eyed with a big grin on his face. This was fun. An adventure. 'No food ever tasted so good,' he said.

Today everything is readily available at the press of a few keys. Cuisine from a choice of continents, that rare recording you want to listen to, the American shirt you're desperate to get your mitts on. But the easier it comes, the less satisfaction it brings. Life's funny that way. Waiting outside Musicland on Ridley Road in the rain for the van to arrive with the latest Jamaican imports? *Schlepping* to the Ivy Shop in Richmond on public transport to get the right colour Harrington? That's the stuff memories are made of. Stuff I wonder if my kids will ever have, as they wander the world looking for the nearest Wi-Fi hotspot.

The kind of freedom we enjoyed back then does not exist now. If it did, it would be branded parental negligence. In the summer holidays we were thrown out of the house after breakfast and told not to come back until teatime. After, that we'd be off again until dark. You could play runouts on a row of demolished houses, bunk in the back door of the local fleapit, take part in an armed robbery at a sub-post office. No one knew where you were or had a clue what you were up to. Essentially, you were left alone to get on with the business of being young.

I cannot say with all honesty that such exploits unfailingly equipped one with all the skills necessary for a happy and successful future life. And I concede that in a face-off, a degree in business studies from a leading university might perhaps bear you in better stead. But they gave you curiosity, a boldness of spirit, an ability to deal with the unexpected. So while I may be no great shakes at spreadsheets and projections, should you ever walk in on a grizzly bear in your conservatory, I'm your man.

Today our kids are GPS tagged and in constant touch via laptops and phones. The constraints on their freedom carefully managed. An adventure is a few days at some festival or another. Large corporate playgrounds with decent facilities, usable toilets and medical care on hand. You can even stay in a fully quipped yurt if you have the dosh. Originally, yurts were a circular tent-like dwelling used by nomadic groups in the steppes of Central Asia.

Now they're where the middle classes hang their hats after a long day's partying, amidst the tasteful comfort of ethnic scatter cushions and decorative throws. If one of my kids ever tells me they're staying in a yurt, they will find a yurt pole lodged firmly where the sun don't shine.

One advantage of tracking and constant communication,

not to mention 24/7 surveillance in many areas, should be a feeling of increased safety and security. And yet quite the opposite appears true. People nowadays seem worried about everything.

I'm sure we had our fair share of rapists, pillagers and paedos back in the day. Crime and violence were part of the fabric of the areas I was raised in. But no one seemed much bothered. Well, not until it affected them personally. Obviously, if you've just been raped and pillaged, it's going to take the shine off your week.

Today we are bombarded with information, most of it worrying or depressing. Because good news is barely news at all. And there is an obsession for awareness. Awareness is one of today's key words. And there's always some cunt trying to raise it. About something or other. For one reason or another. For the most part it seems to me that we are already aware of the things they're trying to raise awareness about. But apparently, we're not quite aware enough. And they won't shut up until they've raised the bar a few notches higher.

But who are these arbiters of awareness? Who is to say what the optimum level is? As each age reinvents its mores and standards, there's an assumption that this time they have it right. That they know better than their predecessors. Which is laughable in its arrogance and dumb as fuck in its lack *of awareness.*

As for me, the battle within rages on. In the red corner my Peter Pannish self. Still plotting places to go, people to see, new worlds to conquer and fun to be had. Opposite are the ravages of time. Make no mistake, they are coming for you. Bobbing and weaving and swinging that clubbing right hand like a young Iron Mike.

This afternoon I made arrangements with my friend

Lucy to go to a Pitchblack Playback of an old Nirvana MTV unplugged session. At these events you sit in a darkened cinema with an eye mask on and listen to the music played very loud. I had been to one with the first Velvet Underground album a while back and it was quite brilliant. The cacophony of noise and discordant feedback at the end of 'Heroin' suddenly sounding very deliberately orchestrated. How had I missed that all these years?

Could be that my buddy Bruno had never slipped me a gummie during playback before, but that's by the by.

Lucy is good company, much younger than me and quite the rock chick. It would be a fun night. I felt good about life.

A few minutes later I got a call from my local hospital. They had arranged a phone consultation with a specialist so I could request another steroid injection in my left knee. The jabs keep the pain at bay and allow me to function somewhere in the proximity of normally. But when I walk downstairs now, I always hold onto the bannister. I then remembered the last time I'd gone to the cinema my friend Jacky had bought tickets close to the back. Walking down towards the screen where the exit was situated after the movie was a tricky old business. It was pretty dark and I had nothing to hold on to. I was scared I was going to fall and bounce all the way down on my arse. It wasn't the prospect of hurting myself that bothered me. It was looking a cunt in front of a bunch of young, hipster cinephiles.

I made a mental note to buy tickets close to the front for my night out with Lucy.

And that's when it happened. A vision flashed into my mind. It was of my late mother in her dotage. Her mobility by then completely shot. She could no longer walk without the help of a frame.

But here's the thing. Mum wasn't walking. She was sitting

in the front row of the cinema. With an eye mask on. Totally lost in the moment as Kurt Cobain belted out the words to 'Smells Like Teen Spirit'.

Tick-tock, tick-tock, tick-tock.

JOHN, I'M ONLY
RIVERDANCING

I was once cajoled by a smooth-talking producer into taking a meeting with Michael Flatley. He of the jigging around like a maniac to unlistenable diddly-dee music while looking like someone had superglued his arms to his sides. I probably shouldn't have gone. But I once wrote a song called 'Ay Ay Ay Ay Moosey', so credibility issues were never uppermost in my thinking.

Flathead lived in a big old drum in Knightsbridge and the maid asked me to take my shoes off when I entered. That gave me the hump from the kick-off. What is the point of a carpet you can't walk on? That is literally the only function the thing had to fulfil. Still, looking around at the plush surroundings, I started thinking if he wants to do some kind of diddly-dee sequel, the four-by-two from Hackney could be just the man for the job.

We were introduced and I couldn't help but notice what a tiny little fella he was. You could sit him on a mantelpiece and he wouldn't stand out amongst the Capodimonte *tchotchkes*. But that's by the by. Flathead started to talk, and boy could he talk. He really liked the sound of his own Hobson's. Now

I'm hardly the silent, moody type myself, but I couldn't get a word in edgewise. It was like he'd ingested the entire planet's coke stash for breakfast. So I just sat back and let him bang on. Amongst the tsunami of verbiage heading my way, I did manage to decipher that he was done with a-dancing and a-prancing and wanted to reinvent himself. Bollocks. Bang goes the Ferrari. And it got worse. He wanted to make an action movie with himself as the star. He talked at great length about what a great James Bond he'd have made. The fact that he was known for Irish dancing and could comfortably fit inside a matchbox he did not view as any kind of disadvantage.

Now there is an unwritten rule that meetings such as this run to around an hour. But it was clearly unread as well. Flathead showed no sign of pausing for air as we hit the two-hour mark. The producer stood up and made his excuses. I got up to leave too, but Flathead gestured for me to sit back down, as he hadn't told me about the film yet. I did as I was told, which left me wondering who was the bigger cunt, him or me.

Over the next hour, I learned that his dream was to star in a film based around the exploits of Hugh 'Bulldog' Drummond. Who? No, Hugh. A gentleman adventurer created by H. C. McNeile, who was very popular in the thirties. Apparently, the time was perfect to reboot the character, and as proof Flathead mimed a bunch of fight scenes for my benefit, right there in his opulent Knightsbridge front room. I sat there staring blankly as he kicked and punched the shit out of thin air. It was like I'd fallen through a hole into some bizarre alternate universe. One where time and connections to reality no longer mattered. Maybe this was it. I was doomed to spend the rest of my life there, like Groundhog Day, but with some mental Irish-dancing midget subbing for Andie MacDowell.

I did escape eventually. After some three hours and fifteen

minutes. With senses battered, I mumbled that I'd see myself out. As I reached the door, I noticed a pair of shoes on the floor. Men's slip-ons. Diminutive and expensive-looking. *The sacred footwear of Flatley.* Probably hand-made by fucking elves. Without further ado, I had them away under my jacket and closed the door behind me. Small payback for what he'd put me through.

Retrospectively, I should have kept them as a souvenir, but as I whistled my way back to Knightsbridge station, full of my newfound freedom, I decided to lob them over a random garden. I smiled as I bade them farewell but resisted the urge to see them off with a celebratory jig.

I never heard another word from the producer or Flathead.

NB. In 2018 Michael Flatley starred in the spy thriller *Blackbird*, which he also wrote, directed and self-financed. It was released in 2022 and reportedly grossed 140,000 Euros at the box office.

THE NAME GAME

It was me who named our first two children, Woody and Nell. Nothing sinister in that. I just happened to suggest names that my wife liked. But it had been noted by the powers that be and when she became pregnant a third time it was made very clear that she would be on naming duty this time around. That was reasonable. Who could possibly argue with that? My second son was born on 8 August, 2000. And my wife announced that she was calling him Ludovic.

'I'm sorry, did you say Ludovic?'

'Yes, Ludovic.'

'But why? What's he ever done to you?'

If you're a Hungarian violinist from the 18th Century or a mad genius who's invented a machine for controlling the world's weather, then I'm sure Ludovic is a perfectly fine and dandy handle. But for a son of mine growing up in East London? Unthinkable. The poor boy wouldn't make it past his first school register.

I tried appealing to my wife's better nature. Forgetting, momentarily, that she'd sold it along with my espresso machine at a car boot sale shortly after we'd married. The lady was not for turning. Ludovic it was and Ludovic it would stay. She stared me down, daring me to argue. I willed myself into silence, biting my bottom lip right down to the big toe in the process.

Maybe I could get used to it. After all, what's in a name? Once it's worn in you probably wouldn't even notice it. You know what these things are like. At my junior school we had a kid who lost a leg in a terrible road accident. When he eventually got out of hospital and came back it was all you could look at, all anyone could talk about. But after a while that all died down. Soon he was just one of the gang again. Good old Stumpy.

A few days later things took a turn for the worse. His mum was taking a bath with him and talking cute in the way that mums sometimes do with new borns. It was quite the beautiful mother and child scene.

And then I heard her call him Ludo.

Ludo?

'Did you just call him Ludo?'

'Yeah. It's cute.'

'It's not cute. It's a fucking board game.'

I was told to get out in no uncertain terms. The most certain term being 'fuck off'. I left in a huff. Which I always kept in the bathroom in case of emergencies.

Soon family and friends began to visit to meet the newest addition to the family. And I noted that while everybody cooed and aahed and said how gorgeous he was, nobody used his name. Not Ludovic. Not Ludo. Not once.

Even my wife's parents avoided saying his name. I thought about trying to enlist their aid in getting her to reconsider her choice but decided against it. They were not my biggest fans. My wife's mother was a devout Irish Catholic. An East End Jew twelve years her daughter's senior was not exactly the son-in-law of her dreams. She was never rude to me or anything like that. But she had her little ways of letting me know how she felt. Like dousing me with holy water and chanting 'The power of Christ compels you' every time she visited.

I'd got off to a bad start with her folks before we'd so much as set eyes on each other. When I first met my wife-to-be she'd had a boyfriend whom she would eventually leave for me. In return for this, he then very generously informed her parents that I'd got her addicted to heroin. Thanks for that. Hell, it seems, hath no fury like a dress manufacturer from North London scorned.

We had to travel to the Midlands where her parents lived to sort things out. I bought her mother a huge, expensive box of Thorntons chocolates. As a nice gesture and to make up for, you know, the whole heroin thing.

I was introduced and handed over the chocolates. Her mum opened them. Unfortunately, it had been hot on the train, and they had all melted. It looked like I had given the woman a big box of shit. At this point I knew it wasn't going to be my day and pretty much gave up trying.

Not having a name to call my son was starting to cause difficulties. I was crazy about him. And, working from home, I was with him 24/7. I had to call him something. When no-one was around, I started to call him Otis. I liked the name, it sounded cool. And Otis B. Driftwood was the name of Groucho Marx's character in *A Night at the Opera*. I'm a big Marx Brothers fan.

You have to understand, this was no cunning plan to usurp my wife's decision. I was far too scared of her for that. It came about by virtue of practicality and desperation. Quite how the name began to spread so quickly is still something

I marvel at. I think Woody overheard me and picked up on it. From then on it was like a mighty river bursting through the walls of a dam. A dam called Ludovic. In truth, I think everyone was so keen to find an alternative I could have called him cheeseboard and still enjoyed their unanimous support. Either way, within days he was Otis. And Otis he remains to this day. It's a good name for the cool kid that he is. It has also proved surprisingly adaptable over the years. When he was learning to swim, he was called Floatis. When he went through his *Game of Thrones* phase he was known as Jon Snowtis. After telling his friends he'd watched his first porno they called him Deep Throatis.

I waited for the expected bust-up with my wife, but it never came. In fact, the matter was never discussed. I think she knew she'd made a bad call and was secretly relieved to have an out.

Years later when we divorced a shopping list of my alleged misdemeanors was bandied about between our legal representatives. Some perhaps justified, others less so. But I have always suspected my capacity for *'man-naming'* was the real reason behind the marital breakdown.

LET'S TALK ABOUT SEX

I was chatting to my friend Lucy recently, and she told me that when she was taking out her rubbish, she had seen a dildo sitting there amongst the black bin bags. 'Someone had just dumped it there,' she said. 'Isn't that weird?'

I agreed that it was weird. 'Maybe they didn't have a recycling box,' I suggested.

Where do sex toys go when they die? I'm always taking stuff to the local landfill.

Imagine turning up with a boot full of your old Lovehoney acquisitions.

'What you got there?'

'Nothing much. Couple of dildos. An old gimp suit. A riding crop and a box of assorted butt plugs.'

'Straight on, mate. Third skip along. Between White Goods and Garden Waste.'

Lu wondered aloud which of her neighbours the mystery dildo had belonged to. I didn't know her neighbours but thought I'd play amateur detective anyway.

'What's it like?' I asked. 'Big,' she replied. 'Strap-on.' *Interesting*, I thought as I scratched my chin and tried to look faintly Belgian. 'I think we could be looking for a recently retired lesbian who's run out of bin bags.' I then paused for effect. 'Or maybe a bisexual.'

'Not necessarily,' she said. 'I've got one somewhere.' I think it was the 'somewhere' that got me. Like owning a strap-on was of such little consequence she couldn't even remember where she'd put it. 'I'm such a scatterbrain. I could have sworn it was at the back of the sock drawer.'

'What are you doing with a strap-on?' I asked.

'What do you think?' she replied, which was no less than I deserved.

Lucy explained that one of her exes had been into pegging and she'd been happy to oblige. She'd enjoyed the feeling of power it gave her.

I spent the next thirty seconds trying to bleach out the image of my petite friend strutting around with an enormous rubber cock. After which I felt both old and naive simultaneously.

I suppose we have a deluge of internet porn to thank for these evolutions of sexual habits. A while back I'd been co-writing a script with a young woman writer. I'd written a scene where the protagonist asks her best friend if she's ever taken it up the bum. 'You can't put that,' said my partner. 'Why not?' I asked.

'Because everyone's done it. No one would bother asking,' I was told.

I remember when anal was the unicorn of heterosexual activities. We'd all heard about it, but no one had ever come across it themselves. Which only added to the mystique.

Eventually, after years of searching and foraging, you might get lucky. But it would take a perfect-storm moment. She'd had a few drinks. You'd just got engaged and put a deposit down on a flat. In joint names. Even then, you'd have to swear an affidavit promising to bang it straight into reverse if she didn't like it.

Now it seems bum action is *de rigueur* for everyone and their mother. Well, maybe not their mother. But then again what do I know?

Some years ago, I met a striking-looking woman named Carrie. She was voluptuous, like a forties starlet. Tattooed and vintage game on fleek, as the kids would say. Do the kids still say that? I have no idea. Our first date was at a bar in Columbia Road Flower Market on a sunny Sunday. Soon after arriving, she told me that she was an alcoholic and couldn't drink. Didn't see that coming, but I appreciated her being upfront. I asked her if she minded if I had a few glasses and she said no, not at all. After that, the conversation flowed easily and I found myself quite taken with her. About an hour in she said she thinks she will have one glass of wine. 'Is that a good idea?' I asked tentatively, trying hard not to sound like the condescending prick I undoubtedly was.

'It'll be fine,' she said.

'Fine' is one of those words that can mean anything. It's the word my kids use to close the convo down when they can't be bothered talking to me.

'How was the exam?'

'Fine.'

'How's the new job working out?'

'Fine.'

'How did it feel to have a visitation from the Archangel Gabriel and be told that you are the new messiah?'

'Fine.'

Here's what probably isn't fine. Fine probably isn't necking a bottle of rosé and getting up in front of a crowded bar to perform an outrageous display of *Dirty Dancing* for the owner's brother. Who, by the way, is paralysed from the neck down and sitting in a wheelchair sucking juice through a straw. No, that probably isn't fine at all.

I only mention this as back story. It's my next date with Carrie I want to tell you about. You're surprised there was a next date? You really don't know me at all. Next to profession in my passport, it says 'crazy woman wrangler'.

I went in hard for the second leg. Dinner at Nobu. She ordered the blackened cod in miso sauce: £38. Similar bit of fish in a Findus parsley sauce: £1.95. Just saying.

But it was a great night. Carrie really was spectacular when she wasn't thrusting her vagina up against paraplegics.

And then she put down her chopsticks, leaned across the table and said she had something to tell me.

'What is it?' I asked.

'I think you should know I can only come from being fucked up the arse,' she replied.

So much for small talk. Suddenly thirty-eight quid for a small piece of fish seemed like a solid investment.

Not long after this, Carrie decided that one tiny cup of sake before we headed back to my place wouldn't do any harm. I thought there was a fairly strong possibility that it might, but didn't say anything. And the evening ended back at the ranch with her touching up my son's girlfriend and then passing out.

I like to think I'm open-minded sexually. But the truth is more that I have zero interest in what other people do in their own time. I'm amazed when anyone gets their PVC knickers in a twist over someone else's sexual proclivities. Generally, I'm more concerned with what shoes someone's wearing.

But I have fond recollections of my formative, adolescent fumblings, and I find myself hoping, probably in vain, that such innocent rites of passage have not disappeared altogether. Amidst all the rampant bumming going on everywhere.

I met my first girlfriend at the Court School of Dancing in Walthamstow, just along from the Granada Cinema. Outside it had a big sign saying 'Walk In – Dance Out', which I and my friends took literally every time we saw it. We'd walk in. We'd dance out. We'd walk back in. We'd dance out again. It never got old.

Every other weekend the Court School of Dancing would have a dance that was open to the public, and that's how I'd met Andrea. She was older than me and worked nearby at the London Electricity Board showroom, which is long gone. It's now a wellness centre and café. Good if you're looking for turmeric, ashwagandha or a kale smoothie. Less handy if you're after something with four hobs and an extractor fan.

I'd go over to Andrea's flat a couple of times a week, and we'd lie on her bed listening to records. Eventually we'd get down to business. Which began with kissing. Hours and hours of kissing. You'd kiss until your lips went numb. Then your entire lower face. You could have had your wisdom teeth out and not felt a thing. Eventually, you'd move on to the holy trinity of teenage boys everywhere. Cloth tit. Real tit. Finger. It was all incredibly exciting. By day I may have been a wholly unexceptional schoolboy. But by night I was an international playboy sex god operating largely in the E17 area. I could never have got through double physics on a Tuesday without the prospect of seeing the lovely Andrea later that night.

As the years rolled by, my eyes were opened to broader sexual horizons, as young men's eyes tend to be. When we hit the band period, they were almost blinded by the light. There was one evening our US record company, Atlantic, took me and David Jaymes out in New York to celebrate the success of our record 'Can You Move'. They had promised us a night to remember. When you're in a band you get a lot of nights to remember, even though you usually can't. We had arrived suited and booted, as was our way when out for a bit of a social, but we needn't have bothered. The club we went to was Plato's Retreat on West 34th Street. We entered into a cavernous expanse replete with cheesy faux-Ancient Greek décor.

There's a bar, restaurant, steam room, whirlpool and several jacuzzis. And a crowded dance floor with some good tunes banging out. The place is packed. There are people everywhere.

And they're all naked. And having sex.

With each other. With themselves. And every combination thereof.

In the restaurant, on the dance floor, in the jacuzzi. Even in the backgammon room. This is a lot to take in. And a lot is certainly being taken in.

There's an artfully designed three-storey multi-chair contraption. Some seats are for giving oral sex. Others for receiving. The middle tier is for greedy bastards who want both simultaneously. I'm told these are now available flat-packed from IKEA.

For the more community-minded there is an orgy room. I check it out. It's a room. And there's an orgy in it. Fair enough.

Dave and I had to disrobe on entry and stand around feeling faintly uncomfortable with our modesty protected by a couple of skimpy towels bearing the club logo. We turn to each other. 'Drink?' said Dave. 'Drink,' I concur.

We make our way to the bar, deftly sidestepping the obstacle course of fucking bodies en route.

'Two beers, please.'

'I'm sorry we're not licensed to serve alcohol,' replies the barman. 'Can I get you some juice?'

His words hang in the air and then float slowly down to the ground unanswered. 'Fuck this,' says Dave. 'I'm not staying here.'

I nod in agreement.

We turn around, walk out and never look back.

These days, as a gentleman of some years, such excitement is strictly anecdotal. I lead a quiet, domesticated existence with my youngest son Otis and more recently his girlfriend Poppi who has moved in with us by stealth. First a head, then a foot, next a spleen. Before I knew it I was waiting to use the bathroom while The Girl From The Barbican – whose parents once sent her to a school for circus skills – did whatever it is such young women do in private. Juggling in the shower or whatever.

Earlier today I glanced out of the window while writing and saw the bin men on their round. They took away our bin bags but left an old mop I had placed alongside them. I went outside and asked them to take it.

'I can't. It ain't in a bin bag,' came the reply.

'It doesn't fit inside a bin bag,' I pointed out. He shrugged. 'If it ain't in a bin bag I don't touch it.'

It occurred to me there are far worse things than mops he could be asked to dispose of. One of which I would have happily inserted up his rear end at that very moment. But being a gentleman of some years, I kept my thoughts to myself and went inside and made a nice cup of camomile tea.

BRUNO AND THE FLY

It's 2016. My daughter Nell and I are sitting on a plane at Luton Airport waiting to take off for Tel Aviv. As the doors close, she notices a fly buzzing around the cabin. She points at it and says, 'His mind is going to be well and truly blown when he gets out at the other end.'

It's 2022. My buddy Bruno has gone walkabout. He lost his missus Jenny this year and is making a fair fist of outrunning his grief. He is here, there and everywhere, and moving at pace. There's a lot of travelling, a lot of flights. Their house in London is up for sale and he's renting a flat in Margate. He walks the beach taking pictures of the sun coming up and then later going down. He doesn't appear to sleep much and arrives everywhere on foot. For a seventy-year-old man, his energy is impressive. The weight has fallen off him and both his beard and barnet have grown longer and more straggly. He looks increasingly like the better-dressed end of cult leaders.

I recently got us tickets to see John Waters at the Barbican. I like the idea of John Waters' movies more than I like the movies. But the man himself is a work of art. When I used to work out the table plan for my fantasy dinner party, I would seat him next to Fran Lebowitz, opposite Groucho

Marx, just along from Christopher Hitchens. I dispensed with such childish imaginings years ago, of course, after the other guests got together and voted me off the table. Chris Eubank abstaining had really hurt.

Bruno got the train down from his coastal dacha but arrived with the air of a man materialising from another dimension. It was good to see him. We've been mates for a long time. Not as long as some friendships we've both had. But enough to have shared respective ups and downs and each have some colour bleed from our palette into the other's.

John Waters did not disappoint. An original thinker with a gossipy side hustle. Funny and smart, catty and caustic. He seemed both bemused and amused by the mainstream acceptance he has ultimately garnered. But he effortlessly held the stage for hours and his disciples were riveted. In the interval, we got chatting to a gaggle of queer Argentinian fanboys who were a lot of fun. Ernesto must have stood six foot six in his wedge-heeled boots, but they set off his leather hot pants and glittery boob tube a treat. There was a time when an interesting-looking audience was part and parcel of the evening's entertainment. It rarely seems to happen any more. People don't make the effort. Or maybe they're just duller people. Either way, Waters' acolytes bucked the trend and the night was all the better for it.

After the show, we had a drink at the Jugged Hare down the road and got talking to the friendly Latvian doorman. Bruno and I are very different, but one thing we share is a penchant for talking to people we don't know. We're both comfortable engaging with all sorts. I think that may be an age and class thing. Living through a lot of change cannot help but broaden your scope and perspective. It's why the best rock stars ever were working class and born in the shadow of World War II. Feel free to discuss this at your leisure.

Catering almost exclusively to the Barbican crowd, the Jugged Hare is a pub less in need of a doorman than any I know. Unless it all kicks off between the David Mamet firm and the contemporary dance posse, but I'm sure that doesn't happen often. The doorman said that suited him. His job was safe and a piece of piss. All he had to do was shepherd smokers into their allotted fourteen centimetres and make sure people didn't take their drinks outdoors and break the licensing laws by enjoying themselves.

Suddenly Bruno announced he was off. I'd assumed he'd stay at my gaff and go back to Margate in the morning. But no. The man who cannot stand still was on the move once again. We said our goodbyes and I watched him walk off into the distance. Walking, walking, walking. Until he faded from sight.

He will have to slow down eventually but for now, if it's working for him it ain't nobody's business but his own. Loss takes a sledgehammer to the being. It is both jagged, searing pain and dull, sickening ache. Unavoidable yet unfathomable. We each have to find our own way through to the other side.

After my old man died, my mum went for grief counselling and ended up training as a grief counsellor herself. Helping others deal with their loss seemed to do her more good than the counselling. My approach was somewhat different. I went to Brazil, got drunk with Ronnie Biggs and fell to bits far from prying eyes. My mum was made of better stuff than me.

Bruno and Jenny had met when they were both teenagers. He was standing outside a bar he was working at in Lloret de Mar, which in the early seventies was the British working-class kids' Spanish destination of choice. Jen cycled past and caught his eye. She held the catch and that was pretty much that. Back in the UK they moved into a one-bed flat above a shop in Woodford Bridge and began their life together. For a time Jen worked at the London Hospital Tavern, a cool East End boozer I also used to frequent. Along with the Camel and the Old Globe, these were seriously fashionable watering holes in their day, full of girls decked out in their finest Miss Mouse and Stirling Cooper and bequiffed young men Ferrying across the Bryan. All these pubs stuck rigidly to the same business model. Hire the best-dressed, best-looking girls to work behind the bar, and they will come. Which they surely did, in their droves.

By 1977 the world had turned. While my life was now immersed in punk and band rehearsals, Bruno and Jenny got married, had a baby and bought their first house.

Which is not to say they led a life of quiet domesticity. Those two always had some verve about them. In the eighties, with one kid in tow and Jenny now heavily pregnant with another, they had relocated to New York after Bruno landed a gig installing fitted kitchens for the Mafia. It's amazing what you could find in the classifieds at the back of the *Woodford Guardian* in those days. One of his customers, Paul Castellano, the boss of the Gambino crime family, got whacked by a henchman of John Gotti while Bruno was on the job at his house. 'They told me to carry on working, so I kept my head down and got on with it. His missus paid me after.'

In later years I remember Bruno and Jenny wanting a super-stylish Italian kitchen for their own gaff. Instead of paying the many arms and legs of top-end retail pricing, they tracked down the manufacturer, hired a truck and drove to Milan to pick it up. They were so nervous of having their precious cargo half-inched, they slept and ate in the truck all the way home. 'The best meal we had was from a little roadside café. Pasta with mozzarella and baby tomatoes. Jen had gone in to get it while I stayed guarding the truck. She even talked them into giving us proper crockery and cutlery.'

IKEA does a very good selection of kitchens at reasonable prices. They also serve a decent Swedish meatball. What it cannot offer you are memories like my friend's.

If Bruno had missed out on anything, I guess it was the hedonistic pursuits of the young, entirely unfettered by responsibility. He'd always been too busy helping pay the rent or mortgage and feeding young mouths. So late in the day, with not much pressing on his to-do list, he's playing catch-up.

He goes to a lot of European music festivals. The kind I always think of as a bit hippyish. He bathes naked beneath waterfalls, dances all night and has developed quite the penchant for hallucinogenics. This has raised a few eyebrows. But I always think one should never listen to an eyebrow.

Bruno went to Meadows in the Mountains in Bulgaria to see a friend of his DJ. It was an eleventh-hour decision, as is his way, and he had set off with a backpack and zero planning. But the pieces had fallen into place, and halfway up a mountain in the middle of nowhere my friend found his idyll. Sunshine, streams, fields, nice people to connect with and round-the-clock music. He had a grand old time. On his last day, he met a bloke from Bristol who gave him a tab of acid. Bingo. According to Bruno, it was amazing and marred only by the fact that 'the trees really didn't like him'. When he left the site at midnight for the flight home, he was still tripping.

He made it to the airport okay and his 6 a.m. flight to London was on time. Before going through customs, Bruno checked his pockets and found a small bag of magic mushrooms he'd forgotten about. Faced with the choice of necking or dumping them, there was only ever going to be one outcome. Down his hatch went the shrooms.

The journey itself was uneventful and Bruno sat back and enjoyed the experience.

The trees may not have liked him, but he got on ever so well with a couple of life jackets and they all promised to stay in touch. He then remembers the pilot announcing they were beginning their descent into Heathrow and it seeming like a really long time before they landed. But hallucinogenics are known to distort one's perception of time, so he put it down to that.

However, this was June 2022. A post-Covid, understaffed time when airlines were showing the world what a shambolic, hopelessly organised, bunch of money-grabbing shysters they really were.

And so it was that Bruno disembarked from the plane, left the airport and found himself in Doncaster. A place he had never before been to nor seen in his life.

At which point his already expanded mind was well and truly blown.

NIGHTCLUBBING

After I jacked in Modern Romance in 1982, I had notions of pursuing a solo career. To make amends to the great British public, if nothing else. But I got caught up in legal problems with the record company and found myself twiddling my thumbs for the next eighteen months while my funds were steadily channelled into my lawyer's new indoor cinema and loft extension. Should you ever find yourself overly encumbered by a surfeit of money, I can wholeheartedly recommend the British legal system to lighten your pecuniary load.

A bored and restless Deane is never a good thing, as anyone who knows me will surely testify. It too often ends in tears. I needed something to do. A diversion if you will. The answer appeared to me as if by Divine intervention – that's the almighty, not the drag queen I would later work with – while casually thumbing through a copy of *The Stage* someone had left lying around in a recording studio. An advert caught my eye. A nightclub in Spain was looking for a singer for the summer season. Somewhere deep inside my head, an involuntary smile began to form.

After I left the band, I vowed to leave all things Latin American behind me. I had a million new directions I was eager to dive into and was done with all that percussion and trumpets malarkey. But this was a nightclub. In Spain. And summer was coming. So I answered the advert, telling them I'd just left a band with a chain of hit singles and would like nothing more than to be their cabaret artiste of choice, performing all my fabulous hits for the pleasure of their no doubt exclusive clientele.

To cut a long story short, I got the job. Go Geoffbeans.

My more grounded friends (okay, friend) did advise me this was not perhaps the most credible move for an artist who still nurtured hopes of a solo career. But I wasn't listening. I thought it would be a bit of a laugh. Something which, retrospectively, seems to have cast the deciding vote in more than a few of my major life choices.

At this juncture, I need to introduce another player in our story: Jim Preen, aka Jimbo.

He was a talented musician who had fallen into owning a recording studio, the Red Shop in Islington, which for years was my second home as I tried out one idea after another. Jimbo was posh, well educated and very funny. I was an idiot council-flat guttersnipe. We were an odd couple with nothing in common but everything. The first time I met Jim he was wearing a tatty striped blazer that looked like he'd found it in a skip. I asked him where he'd got it. 'I found it in a skip,' he replied, and our friendship was sealed. For a few years, Jimbo and I had a lot of fun together. Be it skulking off to dodgy blues parties in Dalston in the early hours. Or pulling two posh Chelsea sorts in the Zanzibar and driving around London with them perched on the back of his old white Merc sports, long blonde hair billowing in the wind, like a scene from a sixties movie. Jim didn't even moan when I painted 'Shave Nelson Mandela' on the front window of his business premises. You can see why I loved the bloke.

Anyways, I told Jimbo about Spain and he immediately

offered to accompany me as my sound engineer. What could possibly go wrong?

As it turned out, almost everything. The Costa del Sol hotspot transpired to be Torremolinos. And the nightclub was a bar with a small stage attached, which served as entertainment to a timeshare apartment complex catering exclusively for Dutch people who looked close to pegging it. By which I mean dying, not the strap-on thing. As open-minded as the Dutch are known to be.

I put my positive titfer on. They had provided us with great accommodation, the weather was beautiful, and the old town served a decent Sexton Blake. It's thirty minutes on stage a night. I can do it with my eyes closed. I'm a professional.

A little back story. In my first band, the Leyton Buzzards, I had learned to deal amenably with all manner of raucous audiences. Save perhaps for the time a skinhead gobbed in the mouth of our bassist as we walked out on stage, and I rammed him in the deuce and ace with the base of my mic stand by way of a considered response.

In Modern Romance things were very different. We had broken the band by driving around the country in a van and bombing into clubs – sometimes arranged, mostly not – and getting the DJ to play a backing tape of the 'Everybody Salsa' twelve-inch. I would sing and rap live while the boys in the band would play percussion and chuck out whistles and streamers to the audience. This rent-a-party *schtick* never failed. Everyone went crazy. That's what got our first record into the charts. Way more fun than TikTok, kids.

After that, we played decent-sized gigs, mainly to enthused young women, which were easy-peasy and not at all unpleasant.

In the US we had a very different career and were super-popular amongst black, Latino and gay crowds. They were sometimes a little taken aback to find the tunes they'd been dancing to were sung by a white four-by-two in a garish pink suit, but it always worked out. Performing at legendary spots like Paradise Garage and Bonds would be the highlight of that part of my life. Proper great days.

So I was seasoned in coping with all sorts. A bunch of Dutch coffin sniffers would not intimidate me. Or so I thought.

The first problem came with my support act. A corpulent, middle-aged German geezer by the name of Rene Volker. He wore a dinner suit on stage and sang a carefully curated set of Tyrolean folk songs and Bavarian bierkeller favourites. The crowd loved him. As he closed his set with a rousing chorus of 'Val-Di-Ree', the old Dutch fuckers sang along at the top of their old Dutch voices. They shouted for more and Volker was only too pleased to oblige. He encored with 'Roll Out the Barrel', by which time I was definitely not having a barrel of fun. As Volker finally left the stage, you could hear the cheers and applause from the luggage-reclaim at Málaga airport. He aimed the smuggest of grins in my direction, which was as close to a mic drop as the human face can manage.

I was performing to a backing tape of Modern Romance hits and decided to attack the crowd full pelt, just like we did in the band's early days.

Except back then there were five of us. Lubricated by alcohol, ambition and each other, itching to strut our stuff before a crowd our own age eager to have a good time. Now I was alone. Stone cold sober and facing a bunch of octogenarian Netherlanders.

It was misery. Jumping up and down and trying to get this party started by yourself is a young man's game. A very stupid young man, at that. The audience just sat there in abject silence. They did not know me nor my songs, and neither did they want to. My confidence drained quicker than the dregs in a drunk's glass. In later life, when my mum was in a care home for elderly people suffering from dementia, I would sometimes accompany her to their monthly disco. The residents there were a more receptive audience than this lot.

By the time the first song finished, I was wishing I was anywhere else on God's green earth. Thirty minutes may not seem long, but inside that building on that night, every second felt like a lifetime. Worst of all were the long percussion breaks, which featured in every tune. In the band we'd bash away on cowbells, pull people up on stage and generally clown around. Always worked a treat. Here all I could do was dance around by myself. Now I've always been happy to hit the dance floor on a night out. But I am no one's idea of a dancer. Least of all with a roomful of oldsters staring coldly at me. I settled into the Jewish wedding one-step, moving my feet from side to side like an embarrassing uncle wholly unfamiliar with the concept of rhythm. With each step, I died a little inside. Only a year and a half before I'd been performing the same songs to huge, adoring audiences in the US. How had it come to this?

Oh yes. I'd thought it would be 'a bit of a laugh'. That's how.

On the second night, half of the audience left before I came on. They clearly had better things to do with their time. Like putting their teeth in a glass of water and emptying their colostomy bags. As Volker and I crossed on stage, he wore a sneer the width of an autobahn.

On night three, the manager of the club informed me he was mixing things up a little. With only two acts at his disposal, that could only mean one thing. From now on I would be the support act to Rene Volker. Oh, the ignominy of it all.

As I stood there trying to process what had happened to my

life, Volker strolled over and draped a heavy, condescending arm around my shoulder. 'No hard feelings,' he said, in an accent that Christoph Waltz would later adopt for his role as SS officer Hans Landa in Tarantino's *Inglourious Basterds*. To be honest, there were quite a lot of hard feelings and I'd have liked nothing more than to have punched him right in the kisser. Val-Di-Ree on that, you fat motherfucker. But discretion being the better part of valour, I resisted the urge and attempted to show some good grace. For the time being, at least.

On the fourth night, a minute or so into my set, the electricity went down. Even the Spanish power grid was against me. With no light and no sound, the oldies began to slowly shuffle towards the exit. The manager, seeing a night's bar takings about to go for a burton, began to panic. He turned to me and Jim and said, 'Do something.'

But what could we do?

Cometh the hour, cometh the Jimbo.

Seizing the moment, he jumped up on the bar and, to the tune of 'The Stars and Stripes Forever', aka 'Here We Go', began to sing 'Amsterdam, Amsterdam, Amsterdam'. I leapt up alongside my friend and joined in, urging everyone to sing along. And they did. What's more, they were enjoying it. The whole place came alive and the bar did a roaring trade. Eventually, the chant started to die down, but fortunately, Jimbo knew his way around Holland and followed up with a rousing rendition of 'Rotterdam, Rotterdam, Rotterdam'.

They loved that too. We had them in the palms of our hands. Next came 'Eindhoven', which was a bit of a leap of faith, but still they sang. By the time we reached 'Maastricht' we were a syllable short and starting to struggle. But suddenly the power came back on and a cheer went up. The manager came over, thanked us for saving the day and gifted us a free bar tab for the rest of the evening. A result of sorts.

The next day, sunbathing around the pool, Jimbo and I reflected on these events and I said it was a shame I'd signed a contract, as I really couldn't face performing again and it would be great to bow out after our short-lived triumph.

'Fuck it,' said Jimbo. 'Let's hire a car and drive to Marbella.'

'But what about the contract?' I replied.

'Fuck it,' said Jimbo. 'Let's hire a car and drive to Marbella.'

This was the kind of legal advice I could get behind.

Jimbo went off to sort the motor, and later that day we did a swift exit from our accommodation. Before we headed off down the coast, we had to stop off at the club to retrieve some bits and pieces I'd left in the dressing room. We stole in like thieves in the night but fortunately, there was no one around.

We found the dressing-room keys behind the bar and let ourselves in. As I collected my possessions, I could not fail to notice Rene Volker's stage tux hung neatly on a peg, alongside, occupying a peg of their own, an enormous pair of white underpants. As if this were not temptation enough, on a nearby table sat a large pair of scissors.

Cutting the arsehole out of a fat German's stage trousers may not have been my finest hour. But I never signed up to be a role model and he'd been asking for it all week. And it was Jimbo who half-inched his pants not me, Miss.

As we sped along the A7 coastal road towards Puerto Banús with its yachts, girls and glamour, Jimbo produced the pants and tossed them out of the window. The sea breeze caught them and the last I saw, they were dancing around in the wind more freely than they'd ever done when wrapped around Rene Volker. Like me, they had been liberated.

BAD NEWS, BAD JEWS
AND A HANDJOB

My Auntie Jinny died in 1998, though she wasn't really my aunt and, come to think of it, her name wasn't Jinny either. She was my nan's sister and the name on her birth certificate was Jane Fairman. But everyone always called her Auntie Jinny and I wasn't one to make waves.

Jinny lived with my nan and grandad their entire married life. She had some kind of mental issue which rendered her childlike at best, and which my dad had diagnosed as being 'twopence short of a shilling'. So they had taken her in and looked after her. In return, she would perform simple tasks like putting the kettle on or making my grandad a ham sandwich at my nan's behest. And my nan did a lot of behesting. The kitchen, or scullery, as it was called back then, was Jinny's domain.

My grandparents also had four children and, to quote a phrase popular at the time, did not have a pot to piss in. So caring for Jinny as well could not have been easy. Fortunately, my grandpa Solly was the most easygoing man you could ever hope to meet and he would do pretty much whatever it took to keep my nan – who was the polar opposite of easygoing – happy. The only exceptions were the odd time he'd lose his wages on the gee-gees before arriving home. On such occasions, you could hear my Nan bellow, 'You fucking useless lazy bastard!' from the downstairs playground, followed by the smashing of crockery against the wall as Solly ducked and dived to avoid said projectiles, which she was aiming with some vigour in his general vicinity.

My nan's temper had a life of its own and was something you did not want to bump into on a dark night or, for that matter, any time at all. In later years, when I was around fifteen, I would experience this for myself. My parents had gone away for the weekend and I was staying with her. At the time my uncle Manny, who was married to my mum's sister Della, had just bought a nightclub in the West End. Before I tell you about that, I should just mention that in later life Manny and Della owned a house which they named 'Mandella'.

Because it's something I feel everyone needs to know.

Manny asked if me and my cousin Tony would go to the club the following night and hang out there to help make it look busy. At two years younger than myself, Tony was only thirteen. But we were both big lumps for our age and both owned tonic mohair suits. We could drink free Cokes all night and hang out at a West End club. What's not to like?

Although there were only a few paying customers within its less-than-hallowed walls, there were a lot of glamorous girls. All of whom were hanging out in a professional capacity. Tony and I didn't twig this. With a combined age of twenty-eight, we were hardly men of the world, so why would we? For reasons I cannot possibly explain, two of the girls came over and sat with us. They were obviously older than us, though they themselves were still young. And extremely pretty, as I recall. We spent the evening with them. Business was never mentioned and they didn't even ask us

178

to buy them any drinks. Yet later that night, in a darkened corner of Uncle Manny's nightclub, shit got very real for me and Cousin Tony with the two girls. Not the full real, you understand. But plenty real for two young idiots like us.

With today's hat on I should acknowledge that as minors we were sexually assaulted and potentially traumatised for years to come. But in 1969 we thought Xmas had come early. It was the most exciting night of our young lives.

The following day I could not wait to call my best friend Neal to tell him all about it. Hey, I was fifteen – give me a break. My nan's phone, whose number I can still remember as Clissold 6854, was one of those beautiful Bakelite models. It sat in her guest room, alongside a wooden cigarette machine full of Embassy Regal ten-packs. Yup, my nan had a working fag machine in her flat. Plenty of people did. Golden days, eh kids?

Nan's guest room, which backed onto her bedroom, was generally considered out of bounds and only ever used for one of three things. Entertaining guests – which she had never done once in her entire life. Storing fried fish – whenever Nan cooked up a big batch of her delicious fried fish (done in matzah meal, the only way), she would always keep it in the guest room to stop people picking at it every time they walked into the kitchen. Its other and most frequent use was as the phone room.

So I was on the dog and bone to Neal regaling him with every colourful detail of the previous evening's exploits. No doubt elaborating and exaggerating along the way, as young idiots are wont to do. When I'd finally milked the story – no ghastly pun intended – for all it was worth, I said goodbye and hung up. At which point my nan came flying out of her bedroom with a face like thunder. She had heard every single, disgusting word I had uttered. 'You dirty little bastard!' she yelled as she proceeded to beat me all around the room with the back of her hand. I laughed as she chased me. Out of nervousness, out of embarrassment and because it was so fucking funny. But my nan could deliver a hefty blow. And that day I signed for quite a few.

Worst of all, she insisted on telling my parents what had happened when they returned. I could have died. However much I had relished labouring over the detail when talking to Neal, she succeeded in topping me.

I presented a case for the defence and asked her why she hadn't walked out of the room earlier, as soon as she'd realised what she was listening in on. She said she had been too shocked to move. Ladies and gentlemen of the jury ... seriously?

I was dreading the lecture from Mum and Dad that would no doubt follow. But it never came. Not another word on the matter was ever mentioned. Well, it was the Swinging Sixties. Maybe they'd passively imbibed some cool and didn't think it was any big deal.

More likely they were even more embarrassed than I was and just wanted it all to go away.

Anyway, where was I? Auntie Jinny. As a kid, we lived just a few doors along from my nan in Eastdown House, part of an estate of council flats in Amhurst Road, Hackney. So I saw a lot of Auntie Jinny. She would often babysit me when my parents went out.

Retrospectively, I suppose one might question the wisdom of leaving your only child in the care of a woman with serious mental health issues. But these were different times. Though having said that, I don't remember anyone else's parents doing it.

The oft-told story about Jinny's condition was that as a child, during the war, she was playing with some kids who had tied her to a tree. The air-raid sirens went off and they had all run away, leaving her there screaming as the bombs rained down over East London. After the air-raid, she was unhurt but never quite right again.

This is the kind of family folklore best filed under B for bollocks. I knew that for sure because of an unusual incident that happened when I was around seven years old, which had shed some light on the situation. Now Auntie Jinny had a very distinctive look going on. She was dark-skinned with incredibly piercing eyes. Her poker-straight, jet-black hair was always cut into a basic elfin crop. Like Mia Farrow's in *Rosemary's Baby*. But there was nothing else remotely elfin about Auntie Jinny. Although short, she was solid. Thick-set, muscular and surprisingly strong. It's true to say of Jinny that once seen, you did not forget her easily.

Which is why it was quite a surprise to pop in to see my nan one day and find two Aunty Jinnys sitting there in the front room. Although dressed differently, they looked identical. Same face, same eyes, same barnet. They even sounded the same when they spoke. I nearly shat myself in shock.

It transpired that the Jinny clone was in fact another of my nan's sisters, Sophia, who was known as Sophie. Maybe she and Jinny were twins. I don't know for sure. And at seven years old, I was no more qualified to offer an accurate diagnosis of Sophie's condition than my dad had been of Jinny's. But even to a kid, it was obvious that whatever Jinny had, Sophie had the same. And you didn't get it from being tied to a fucking tree.

Sophie was the worse version of Jinny. Whereas Jinny had been taken in by my nan and become socialised, Sophie had been sent off as a child to an establishment known as the Metropolitan Asylum for Chronic Imbeciles in Caterham, which had been set up in 1870 to house 'certain categories' of the sick from poverty-stricken areas of metropolitan London.

And that is where the poor woman had spent her entire life.

My nan, a tough old broad with a kind heart, must have arranged for Sophie to have a home visit, and she stayed for a week. Maybe Nan was testing the waters to see if she could manage both of them. I wouldn't put it past that jumbled contradiction of a woman. Either way, it didn't work out. Sophie resented Jinny for living with my nan. Jinny felt insecure that she was being usurped. The two women hated each other.

Matters reached a head when Nan heard a loud thump from Jinny's bedroom and upon investigation found Jinny on the floor, legs and arms protruding from beneath a wardrobe that Sophie had pushed over onto her. Help was called to free Jinny, and Sophie was shipped back to Caterham and never heard of again.

After Nan and Grandad died, Jinny was looked after in a care home. My mum had by then morphed into her own mother, part of which meant an inherited responsibility towards her aunt. She never missed a week visiting her which, let's be honest, couldn't have been much fun. And she always made sure Jinny had everything she needed.

'Doing anything today, Mum?'

'Just popping out to buy Jinny some new drawers.'

'Lovely. You enjoy yourself.'

It was mum who told me that Auntie Jinny was very poorly and things didn't look good. I visited her in the hospital and she thought I was Paul Gascoigne. She was clearly on her last knockings, so I let it slide. Otherwise, I'd have suggested a kick-around in the car park.

I went to see her with another relative of mine, Cousin Stephen. He noticed that her lips were dry and sat there kindly feeding her sips of water from a tumbler. After a few minutes of this, I pointed out the large *Nil By Mouth* sign above her bed. He got really panicky that he'd done something terrible, which amused me no end. After she passed away, I would ask him repeatedly if he thought it was him that had killed her. He would tell me to fuck off. We were a close family, that way.

Jinny's funeral took place on a miserable, rainy day in a Jewish cemetery in Waltham Abbey. My mum asks me to look over the eulogy she'd written. I do as she requests and tell her she cannot open with the phrase 'Jinny was a retard'. She replies, 'But Jinny was a retard.' I back off. This is no day for giving notes to a difficult writer.

As Jinny had outlived most of her contemporaries, the ceremony is sparsely attended.

This creates something of a problem. At a Jewish funeral the head mourner has to say '*kaddish*', a prayer for the dead spoken in Hebrew, just before the coffin is lowered into the ground. There are precious few heads present, let alone a head mourner. So the rabbi asks me if I would say the *kaddish* prayer. Frankly, I'd have rather had a rusty spike stuck up my arse, but I agree, as he looks extremely holy and I don't want to incur the wrath of the almighty, or, for that matter, my mother.

I should point out that I can just about read Hebrew. I was taught it as a kid. And I have said this prayer before when I buried my own father. But this is still not a performance I am much looking forward to. The rabbi says he'll give me the nod at the point where I have to come in, and I say, 'Cool bruv, sorted,' or words to that effect.

The ceremony begins. I open my prayer book and reach into my jacket pocket for my glasses. Shit. They're on the kitchen table. Which, as it happens, is not in my jacket pocket. I look down at the prayer book and am met by a misty grey blur. Without my glasses, I cannot read a newspaper headline, yet alone a tiny ancient Aramaic-based text running from right to left. I am to all intents and purposes a blind man. I start to panic. It's brass monkeys out but I'm sweating buckets. I consider doing a runner, but before I know it, the rabbi looks at me and gives me the nod. I remain silent. Sweaty and silent. All eyes are on me ...

I can offer no real explanation for what happened next. There was no eureka moment. No light bulb suddenly appearing above my head. Just a seamless segue into the desperately absurd. I begin to rock. Not like AC/DC, but back and forth. Rhythmically. Like documentary-film footage of Hassidic Jews at the Wailing Wall. It is a motion that says, 'I am a Jew. Look at me, I am doing Jew stuff.'

And the boy is off at a canter.

I then throw in some mumbling. Low, fast, indiscernible mumbling. In time with my rocking. Every now and then and I mix things up with a sequence of guttural throaty noises. Now they sound really Jewish. I take a quick glance around. All good so far. Now I really hit my stride. This is exhibition stuff. Imagine, if you will, a flamboyant performance of completely meaningless gibberish intended to embody the entire history and spirit of an ancient religion. Baby, I owned that *kaddish*.

Looking up momentarily, I notice my cousin Stephen, who has turned up to pay his respects. His mouth is wide open and an expression of abject disbelief is making its way slowly across his face. He knows exactly what I am doing.

He throws me a look and shakes his head in disapproval. I return serve with a look of my own.

One which says 'Okay, so I'm blagging it. But at least it wasn't me that fucking killed her.'

WHAT CAN I GET YOU?

My buddy Bruno, who has gone walkabout, ran a hole-in-the-wall pop-up bar every Sunday in East London's Columbia Road Flower Market. It's a vibrant area that sees a wonderful flow of people from all over the world, as well as a core of locals. I'd pop down to see Bruno most Sundays, enjoy a sherbet or two and soak up the vibes. When the weather's on your side, there's no cooler spot in London to hang out. Entertainment would be provided by old Jonnyboy Moore the busker, in his sharp suit and matching trilby, who would croon his way through a set of swing classics. 'If you're happy, tell your face,' he'd crack wise to the gathered crowd as the hat was passed around. Actually, there was no hat. It just made the sentence more evocative. These days it's a Zettle machine for contactless card payments. Welcome to the new East London.

I didn't like seeing the bar closed. It felt wrong. So I offered to run it for my friend while he was away. He said yes, tossed me the keys and so began my Sunday side hustle.

During the week I'd been working on this book and a couple of film scripts. This involves spending a lot of time alone. And I'm not the kind of writer who prefers his own company. No isolated cottages in the wilderness for Mr

Deane. You will never find me in the kitchen at parties. I like people, always have. So running a busy bar one day a week made perfect sense to me.

I've always enjoyed the interactions of London's street markets. I still shop for food at Hackney's Ridley Road when I can, as my late mother and grandmother had done before me. Walking around, the memories come thick and fast from every which way. As a kid, sneaking looks through the gates of the *shechita*, the kosher slaughterhouse, to watch the headless chickens run around like headless chickens. The colours and smells of Caribbean fruit, veg and spices. Now commonplace but then something new and wonderful. Like the sounds of Prince Buster or Bob and Marcia emanating from the record shop, they added gloriously to the life force of the area as new immigrant communities so often do. I feel so lucky to have grown up in that place at that time. I would have used the word 'blessed', but then I'd have to kill myself. So we'll stick with lucky.

I remember the time my Auntie Bessy had a function to go and needed a new dress. Now Auntie Bessy was a big woman. A very big woman. My kids refuse to believe me, but I swear when she eventually passed away, they had to get a JCB to lower her casket into the ground. So buying an evening dress off the peg for Bessy was a complete non-starter. And the cost of having such a garment made, not to mention the difficulty of getting her to fittings, was also prohibitive. Mum was gifted the task of sorting out this extraordinary wardrobe conundrum. After a period of head-scratching, something she saw on TV triggered an idea.

Off we went to Ridley Road and, following some arbitrary haggling with one of the many *schmutter* merchants you would find there at that time, Mum returned home with a very large roll of fabric under her arm. This was delivered to a friend of hers with a sewing machine.

And so it was that several weeks later, inspired by Demis Roussos, a thirty-four-stone Jewish woman would attend a bar mitzvah wearing the world's biggest floral kaftan. My old man said she looked like Kew Gardens had grown legs.

The Jews and Jamaicans in the market have mostly gone now. It's mainly Asians and Africans. Different but the same. The smell of freshly baked rotis fill the air. A matriarch, stunning in her jazzy boubou, barks demandingly at the Indian fishmonger before handing over a fiver for a bag of mackerel. The place is alive in the truest sense of the word. You can feel the energy around you course through your veins. And you don't get that at Waitrose, baby.

As a teenager, I'd had various stints working in the markets. I flogged whistles to Nigerians in Brick Lane and fly-pitched Clackers out of a suitcase. Clackers, for the uninitiated, were two solid plastic balls joined together by a small piece of string. With some practice, you could agitate the string and make said Clackers hit each other repeatedly at such a speed they would blur to the human eye. A fairly pointless pursuit, you might think. And you'd not be wrong. As an added bonus, this would also make the most annoying clacking sound on God's green earth. I can sense you're still not impressed. But in 1969 people had grown tired of sitting around waiting for TikTok to be invented and Clackers were all the rage.

As luck would have it, I was rather a dab hand with them and as I displayed my artistry, crowds of people would gather around and stare in wonder. I was making money hand over fist. Well, I did for a week or two. By week three, pissed-off punters were turning up with bruised and swollen forearms demanding their money back.

PUNTER: Look what they did to my fucking arm!
ME: Did you not think to stop doing it, mate?

The scene ends with me legging it down the road, suitcase half open, Clackers rattling in the wind.

I like the early mornings at Columbia Road, seeing the market come to life. Every plant, flower and herb you can imagine being arranged into attractive displays. Traders stocking up on beigel-shaped carbs for the day at the café with the worst spelling in the entire postcode.

I pick up my sack of ice outside the Lord Nelson pub from a man with a limp, known only as Iceman. That's the bloke, not the limp. I sling it over my shoulder and head back to the bar. I always wear a naval bib and brace for the market and at this point feel like a proper working man. Okay, so the bib and brace is by Nigel Cabourn and set me back four hundred quid, but I do look the part.

The most popular drink I sell at the bar is a Bloody Mary. After some highly enjoyable experimentation, I settled on a blend of some nineteen ingredients. The customers have played their part in its evolution. An Italian woman suggested I try a splash of extra-dry vermouth. Pickle juice came courtesy of an Australian surfer dude. I had trouble buying it so I started brewing my own. And it was a Cuban couple who suggested the umami punch of a few drops of Maggi seasoning. If nothing else, film writing has taught me the value of a collaborative process. My own masterstroke was a pinch of Greenfields Himalayan Pink Salt with Chilli and Lime and a sprinkle of smoked paprika. But keep that to yourself. All in all, it is a very palatable tipple.

I'm starting to see some of the same faces return every week, keen to start the day with their regular livener. I like that. I've even had American tourists seek me out following recommendations from fellow countrymen who'd visited me previously. One such chap was a giant of a man who looked like he had to be an American football player or a wrestler. He had come to the market straight from the airport to try my Bloody Marys. And try them he did. Four sunk back to back inside a minute or two, each with an added double shot of vodka. He then walked around the corner where my son Otis, who is a band manager, also shucks oysters every Sunday. He demolished a dozen of his finest bivalves in record time before returning to me for one for the road. This was early in the morning and peak summer, when it was already scorching hot. 'I expect you'll be checking into your hotel and crashing out for the rest of the day,' I offered in the way of conversation. 'No, man,' he replied, 'this is a pitstop. I have to get the train to Manchester now.' My heart went out to his fellow passengers.

I serve a lot of daughters who moved to London for work whose mums are visiting for the weekend. I love them. Mum's eager to take in everything the city has to offer in her short stint in the smoke and cannot wait to tell you all about her beautiful offspring's career achievements. Daughter rolls eyes in the background and chugs back another Aperol Spritz to anaesthetise herself from the embarrassment.

There's a couple in the deepest throes of young love, only she lives in Hackney and he in Brooklyn. They save and visit and only have eyes for each other and their respective airports. And a motley collection of the red of eye looking for a hair of the dog that gnawed its way through to the bone. Japanese fashion students who look a million dollars and club together to raise the funds for a communal glass of Sangria. The dealers who always pay cash and the tech start-up Europeans, who prefer the Apple watch.

'Do you take card?'

'I take card, cash, jewellery, and attractive blonde children suitable for resale.'

'Can I get a vegan Bloody Mary?'

'Of course. But it will involve going somewhere else.'

'Do you have anything for someone who doesn't drink alcohol?'

'Ketamine?'

Last Sunday a quietly spoken middle-aged Israeli chap ordered a Bloody Mary from me. He paid and left but returned a quarter of an hour later. 'My father always drank Bloody Marys,' he said. 'He would mix them himself in his special way. I drank my first one ever with him. After I left home, whenever I visited him, he would always make us both one. We lost my dad eight years ago. As soon as I tasted the first sip of your drink, I saw him standing there. It was the same taste. Thank you for that.' And then he turned and walked away.

Love, life, humanity. You find it in the most unexpected places.

DOWN TO MARGATE

Head down, walking briskly through Westfield Stratford City. The stench of Cinnabons and minimum wage in the air. I loathe this place. It speaks of phone shops and laptops and trainers. Cheap clothes made by cheaper children. If Dante had come here to buy his underwear, he'd have written about the ten circles of hell.

A pretty girl is massaging the shoulders of a fat man whose arse looks like it's about to ingest the chair he's sat upon. She works hard on him. But it's futile. A bomb could go off on that neck and he wouldn't feel it. I imagine her whipping out a razor and slitting his throat. No happy ending for you today, fatso.

I pass through the World Food Court. Any resemblance to the world or its food is fleeting. Flaccid production-line sushi. Street food in search of a street. An array of restaurant frontages compete for your attention and contactless payment. Some of the names are vaguely familiar. Eateries perhaps once worth visiting. Now rolled out and facsimiled into gastronomic oblivion. Westfield – where good food goes to die.

It's not just what it is that I hate. It's where it is. Stratford has always been a poor working-class area. And it still is. This hedge-fund hellscape is a finger jammed into an open wound. All that talk of regeneration surrounding it and the Olympics. No one believed it then or mentions it now. The only things regenerated around here were the contents of corporate coffers.

My friend Sash da Bash used to own a cool little clothes shop not far from me in Woodford, which is four stops away from Stratford on the Central line. A former DJ, he had a good eye for Stüssy tees and always played cool tunes. Sash, a four-by-two heavily into meditation, had been around the block a few times and was a friendly, interesting bloke to spend time with. He and his shop quickly became part of the community. They added to life in the area. And it did well enough to support him and his family. Within a few years of Westfield opening, he'd gone bust. God knows what it was like for those with businesses close by.

A few doors along from Sash's gaff was Little Fat Scott's barber shop. LFS, as he was known, ran the kind of place you'd walk into for a haircut and leave with a case of wine or a Fortnum's hamper. Proper old-school. Every year he would throw the Scotting Hill Carnival on the pavement outside his shop. He'd get Jerk Donald in to cook up a storm on the barbecue, buckets of Red Stripe on ice, Lee Perry blaring out. LFS and Sash da Bash were old mates and their two shops formed quite the social hub.

Back in 2011, when the riots were kicking off, word went around that Sash's shop was going to be hit that night. Shops to the left and right had been looted the previous evening, so the threat was taken seriously. Phone calls were made and a bunch of solid citizens agreed to assemble and defend the premises should it prove necessary.

I went along with my eldest boy, Woodrow. He'd just turned eighteen and had insisted on coming. I wasn't happy about exposing him to possible violence, but know a rite of passage when I see one and had not stood in his way.

We met at LFS's gaff, and walking in we were greeted by an array of weaponry on reception that would not have disgraced the Krays and Richardsons in their prime. Baseball bats, hammers, cleavers and an axe. Scotty then disappeared into his stockroom and returned with a fearsome-looking blowpipe and a box of darts, which he was keen to demon-strate to the gang. Three puffs of breath later there was a line of darts embedded in the wall just above the display of assorted waxes and pomades. I was taken aback by his prowess. Where the fuck had he learned to do that? Despite his shortness of stature, LFS was too fat and Jewish to be a Pygmy.

Woody and I agreed to take the first shift patrolling out-side. This entailed us walking a couple of hundred yards in opposite directions and then doubling back to cross each other for the next half hour or so. If all this is starting to sound like well-organised armed resistance, I owe you an apology for what would be an entirely erroneous impression. To get a clearer picture, I should give you the full SP on the vigilantes involved that night. There was Sash da Bash and LFS who, despite their eccentricities, were both nice Jewish boys.

Another four-by-two present and correct was a barber who worked for Scott, name of Jake Fugler. Also known as Jakey Feigele. *Feigele* is a Yiddish word that literally means 'little bird'. But it's more commonly used as a good-natured term for an effeminate homosexual. Jakey Feigele was not a homosexual, effeminate or otherwise. But Fugler sounded enough like *Feigele* for the name to stick.

Jakey used to smoke a lot of strong weed. He would end up living in Cambodia largely for that reason, I suspect. He once returned to the UK for a visit and swore blind he had been kidnapped and held captive in a cage in the jungle by gangsters who planned to sell his organs. He had escaped and was found naked and terrified in a nearby village. We all put it down to a psychotic episode on account of the weed. And because we couldn't see there being enough of a market for the Feigele's organs to warrant all that effort.

Viking Will, who owned a nearby trainer shop and stocked an excellent range of Vans was also amongst our numbers. Will could have given Chris Hemsworth a run for his money as the Norse god of thunder and looked like he could handle himself in a scrap. He was the bloke to stand behind if it kicked off. Then there were four lovely Cuban lads who worked at a local restaurant. They were always smiling and also enjoyed a spot of puff. It's conceivable these two things were not entirely unconnected.

After thirty minutes no one had come out to relieve us, so we went back into the shop.

LFS had put on some reggae and Feigele and the Cubans were skinning up. Sash was also doing his bit for the cause by passing around glasses of rum. This was not exactly the Stern Gang.

The boys had got bored sitting around and decided to render the proceedings more enjoyable. In the end, no looters showed up and we spent the night talking, laughing and getting wasted. At one point two coppers walked in and saw the arsenal still on display through a dense fug of marijuana smoke. LFS began to spout some half-cocked explanation but the older of the two Bills showed him the hand. 'We really don't want to know,' he said with a smile. After which they turned around and walked off without another word. Now that's my kind of policing.

All of which was a far cry from where I now find myself.

If I came across any looters in Westfield, I'd probably hold the door open for them.

So what am I doing here? Nothing to do with shopping or eating, that's for sure. My buddy Bruno who went walkabout has resurfaced in Margate and I'm popping down to see him. The train leaves from Stratford International, which is the quietly tucked away, poor relative of the main Stratford station. The link joining the two is Westfield.

I arrive at the station ahead of schedule enough to catch an earlier train. The barriers won't let me through and the ticket inspector tells me my ticket is off-peak so I'll have to wait for the one I'd booked. That all makes perfect sense and he's only doing his job, but I still want to punch him in the face. Instead, I smile and thank him and get myself a double macchiato to pass the time.

Sitting in the soulless station concourse is a man playing show tunes on a piano. His life certainly is a cabaret, old chum. They've become quite the thing, these public pianos. There was one in Queen's Hospital, Romford when my mum was on what seemed like her last legs. Broken hip, pneumonia and advanced dementia. As it turned out, the old woman also had a hidden stash of legs and pulled through. But hospital visits where one knows it may be the last time you see a loved one alive are a special kind of hell. Having a shithouse version of 'Candle in the Wind' as the soundtrack doesn't make it any easier.

Finally allowed onto the platform with my off-peak povvo ticket, I caught my train and sat close to an Orthodox Jewish couple in their forties who were both working on laptops. Mrs Orthodox Jew was extremely attractive. She wore a *shei-tel* which is a traditional wig intended to symbolise modesty after marriage. Her real hair being reserved for her husband's eyes alone. I've never understood why concealment of the barnet is considered commensurate with virtue. I'm sure there's the occasional hair fetishist out there, but they're few and far between. And in any case, this *sheitel* looked expensive and well-styled. If anything, it served to enhance her good looks. She was one hot-looking Orthodox Jew.

Two of my favourite foods are Ibérico ham and *cochinillo asado* – roast baby suckling pig – and I haven't been inside a synagogue for over thirty years. So I'm already a bad enough Jew without sitting on a train fantasising about the Orthodox babe sitting opposite me. But the mind wants what the mind wants. It's not as though you have any control over these things. More likely there's a degree of the elephant in the room at play. Except in this case, the elephant is about forty-two, well fit and to my way of thinking enjoys crawling around on her hands and knees in expensive French underwear.

Her husband's eyes meet mine. He gives me a friendly smile that disarms me and makes me feel bad for my lascivious thoughts, which up until then I had been thoroughly enjoying. I consider trying to work him into the scenario as a compensatory gesture, but decide a Hassidic cuck is a step too far even for me. So I put on my headphones and turn away, pretending to be suddenly engrossed by the view from the window.

I look for something to listen to on my phone and settle on a podcast about the beef between different factions of the trans and LGBTQ communities. It begins by clarifying terminologies and explains the difference between gay men, queer men and same-sex-attracted men. My head's already spinning and the trans wallahs haven't even turned up yet. I decide to veto education in favour of entertainment. I switch podcasts and relisten to Gilbert Gottfried talking to Bob Einstein back in 2016. Einstein's better known in the

UK as Larry David's friend Marty Funkhouser in *Curb Your Enthusiasm*. As himself, he's foul-mouthed, vulgar and prone to trampling over more delicate sensibilities. He's also hilarious. His reminiscences of Bill Cosby taking an hour out of his working day to 'teach comedy' to young Asian models are worth the admission price alone. Both men are sadly now brown bread. So many of the artists I like are. Each one a marker of your own mortality. But I don't think or worry about dying. My perfectly holistic lifestyle has stood me in good stead so far and I see no reason for that to change any time soon. And if you've never come across irony before, tip your hat and say hello to the previous sentence. I never caught Covid. Not even once. I had every injection that was offered. What kind of *schmuck* wouldn't? But beyond that, I didn't go to any great lengths to stay safe, and broke rules as and when it suited me.

My theory is the Covid germs took one look at me, saw what my body had survived over the years, and decided I wasn't worth the hassle.

Writing this, I'm reminded that in the beginning it was called Corona. Remember that? Who names a deadly virus after a light Mexican beer? No wonder it never stuck. Our government had no idea about marketing. Look at the fella they used to wheel out to tell you what you had to do to stay safe. Professor Chris Whitty. You want me to listen to wellness tips? Show me a healthy-looking dude with a tan. Not someone who looks like Death from Bergman's *The Seventh Seal* on his day off.

Talking of days off, the train pulls into Margate and I alight. Outside the station, the sun is shining, there's a strong sea breeze, and no Uber or Free Now on the dog and bone. I am definitely not in Kansas any more. A fact further reinforced by a mini-cab driver who doesn't have Waze and has trouble finding the steering wheel, never mind the hotel I'd booked. On our third lap around, he is still asking me, 'Is it down here? 'Should I turn left?' I don't know, mate. I'm a guest, I don't own the fucking gaff. I was rather hoping you'd know where it is. What with you living here and being a cab driver and all.

Eventually we stumble across it more by luck than judgement. I get out, check in, and set off to meet my friend for a few sherbets before lunch. As I enter the bar, I see Bruno. The weight has fallen off him since we last met and his beard is even longer and wilder. But for a man who has spent almost a year on the move since losing his wife Jenny, he looks well enough. Somewhere between Rick Rubin and a crazy hermit living alone in a log cabin.

I'm pleasantly surprised to see his son Oyster Boy sitting with him. Nothing cryptic about the handle, by the way. He sells oysters for a living. In East London's Columbia Road and Broadway Market, as well as upmarket functions and other prestigious events. I think it may have been me that bestowed said moniker upon him. He might dispute that and if he does, I'd be happy to concede. I'm not in this life for glory or posterity and he's a fiery sort, younger and stronger than me.

The bond between our families is strong and my friendship with Oyster Boy has grown to one independent of the one I have with his father. He's intelligent and funny, with something of the Wildling about him. I once saw him arrive late to work at Columbia Road on his bike wearing just a pair of jeans. No shirt, no shoes and socks. He had to borrow a pair of shoes from Pablo, who ran the bar opposite him.

'Big night?'

'Yeah, man.'

The boy left London a while back and now resides in Hastings/St Leonards. My son Woody has settled further afield in Lisbon. Both are doing well, but I cannot help think-ing it's London's loss. They are cool, interesting, ambitious young working-class men. The kind that should be the life-blood of our capital. In the end, it comes down to economics, which is always a monumental drag.

I love London. This city is ingrained on my being. And I have never had a problem with change. Outsiders have, and always will be welcome here. We are a city forged from out-siders. But I have misgivings about what it's evolving into. If young people who were raised in our traditions have to leave, what becomes of its essential character? Some will tell you that went years ago. Racist grandads and the like, who frankly can go fuck themselves. But when people like me are starting to worry, it is perhaps worth listening to.

The agenda for the first part of the day was drinking, walking and talking, and we did plenty of each. Margate – or Margitt, as my nan used to call it – is Britain's original seaside town. When I was a kid, it was *the* destination for working-class people who wanted a few days at the coast. Seafood stalls, donkey rides, teeth-destroying sugary rock, and Dreamland. What more could you ask for? In the sixties it was also a favoured venue for the annual bank-holiday barney between mods and rockers.

You can probably trace the start of its decline back to the seventies, when the package holiday opened up foreign climes to working people. A tub of whelks could not compete with the saffron-tinged glamour of the paella, and holidaying at the English seaside came to be seen as the downmarket option for those that couldn't afford better. In later years, the blight of the out-of-town retail park and shopping centres robbed Margate of vital commerce, and its spiral down-ward was expedited. As little as ten years ago a black cloud hung over the town. Run down, with high unemployment.

Dreamland – a beacon to happier times – fell into disrepair and eventually closed. 'It was depressing here,' one long-term resident I chatted to told me. 'Even the junkies were moving out.'

And then something began to happen. Something I have seen before in the poorer parts of East London.

We had left the area I was raised in when I was a teenager. My parents wanted a better life for us and could not wait to get out. Too many bad memories. Soup kitchens and poverty. But my heart had never left the East End. I didn't feel right anywhere else.

When places are forgotten and neglected, they become cheap to live in. And if those places enjoy other advantages – such as an otherwise great location in a capital city, or in Margate's case, the sea, other people start to move in. Often young people with a creative or artistic leaning. Types who are perfectly happy to live amongst often large immigrant communities and don't give a fuck if there isn't a Waitrose nearby.

In the eighties I moved back to Bethnal Green, where the shoots of something special were starting to grow. I lived in Minstrel Court, which was an old Victorian school close to the flower market. My neighbours were all young and none had kids. There was a stand-up comic, an up-and-coming TV producer, a model, a gang of roadies, Alice Rawsthorn, a design journalist from *The Times*, who was also a banging Northern Soul dancer, and graphic designer Steve Howell, who drove the coolest old Citroën DS I had ever seen and is still a good mate to this day. For a time Bobby Gillespie from Primal Scream lived on the ground floor. I swear the geezer only had one shirt. He'd take it to the dry cleaner's and walk home bare-chested.

This was part of the beginning of the gentrification of East London which today, forty-odd years later, sees it *the* destination of choice for young people the world over. I don't much like the term gentrification. For a kick-off, most of the residents of Minstrel Court were born working class. There was nothing gentrified about them. They were just cool.

This kind of rejuvenation was the polar opposite of what happened with Stratford. It was gradual and organic and powered by people. An area refreshing itself. And this is exactly what happened – and is still happening – in Margate. Walking around, I could not help but notice the lack of chains and big high-street names. It was one independent shop, bar and restaurant after another. People shopping and socialising at their neighbour's businesses and putting money in each other's pockets is the perfect foundation for a community. Everywhere we stopped, people knew Bruno and chatted with him. It was easy to see what he liked about the place.

He showed me the Oval Bandstand, where the Libertines had played recently. Anyone who knows me is aware that I am an inveterate fanboy and the Libs had long counted as one of my favourite bands. The notion of them playing a small outdoor gig for locals filled me with deep joy.

The band has strong connections to the area. They own the Albion Rooms hotel and recording studio and sponsor Margate FC. Carl Barât and his partner Edie Langley also opened the Love Café, which features music, comedy and poetry. It's hard to think of two more unlikely allies of the local tourist board than Barât and Pete Doherty, but their association has undoubtedly added to the town's growing cachet.

There are a few who don't like the changes and resent the influx of newcomers. There always are. Some years back I visited a mate who had moved to Hastings, where something not entirely dissimilar was going on. We sat outside a pub having a drink and a catch-up, and he was telling me about a new art gallery that had opened on the Stade, a beach by the old town that has been a working fishing port for over a thousand years. Some dome head sitting close by stood up and walked over to our table. 'It's cunts like you that have ruined this place,' he said angrily before storming off. No doubt heading home to knock the wife about a bit before teatime.

We walked around for hours before deciding we needed to eat. Bruno directed us to a restaurant he liked, where we rested our lallies and gave the menu the once-over. It was good to spend time with these two again. It had been too long. The conversation and wine flowed easily over a fine turbot lunch. There was a lot of laughter, a healthy proportion of which was down to a story relayed by Oyster Boy of a recent exploit. If you have a minute to spare, I'd like to share it with you.

On his forearm, the boy has a tattoo of a life ring emblazoned with the words 'save yourself'. Some time back it occurred to him that having a real life ring bearing the same slogan on the wall of his abode would be a very cool thing indeed. You, of course, do not know Oyster Boy, but I can testify that this is very much the kind of thing he might think.

One night while driving home, he passes some roadworks that have been cordoned off. The works have caused some water displacement and because of this, there is a life ring on site. Oyster Boy pulls over and gets out to inspect the situation further. He walks through the water, which he swears does not reach above his ankles. 'Basically, it was a puddle,' he explains. Reasoning that the life ring is only there to conform with some ridiculous health-and-safety requirement and would never actually be needed to save a life, he decides to half-inch it. This distinction is important. He might be a tea leaf, but he is a civically minded one.

He gets the life ring home, and away from the cover of darkness he now sees that it is shiny and brand-new looking. Not at all what he had in mind for his proposed *objet d'art*. So it is thrown into a cupboard and forgotten about.

Many months later Oyster Boy is again out driving and again comes across a life ring. Upon further inspection, he sees that this one is of vintage provenance and just what he had been looking for. It is perfect. There is a problem, though. It's by a large lake to be used in case of emergency. And the chances of someone needing a life ring in a lake are considerably higher than in a puddle. And our man has principles. So he does not take it.

Instead, he decides to go home and get the first life ring then drive back to the lake and swap them over.

The first part of his plan goes well enough. But when it comes to removing the life ring from its housing, he discovers that it's connected to it by a thick rope. Furthermore, there is a second rope tethering it to a hook embedded in the ground. And try as he might, Oyster Boy cannot untie the ring from the ropes. He produces his trusty oyster knife and starts to cut his way through. But while they have a sharp tip, such knives are not made for cutting. It's a long, arduous job. Finally, after much effort, the ring is liberated. He removes it and attempts to replace it with the other one. But it is a little smaller than the original and the two pegs it should sit on are too far apart for it to fit. At this point, one might think he'd just leave it there and do a bunk. But Oyster Boy is not the kind to leave a job half done. So he fetches a screwdriver from his van and sets about removing and refitting the pegs to take the new ring.

It is by now pitch-black out. Engrossed in the task at hand, he suddenly sees two lights heading toward him. As they get closer, the forms of two uniformed men become visible. They introduce themselves as forest rangers in charge of the area. The lights are torches in their hats so that they can see in the dark. Something I feel milliners everywhere should take note of. Who would not want a hat with a torch on it?

One of the Rangers asks Oyster Boy what he is up to. Thinking on his EU size forty-fours, he explains that he is in the employ of the local council and has been sent to replace the old substandard life ring with a brand spanking-new one. Miraculously the ranger is pleased to hear this and tells Oyster Boy he had previously written to the council on this very matter. I understand the phrase 'not fit for purpose' is bandied about not infrequently during the conversation which ensues. The boy cannot believe his good fortune. Ranger number two is perhaps not quite as convinced as his colleague and suggests that this is a rather late hour to be out on council work.

'To be honest, fellas, it was on my list of things to do this morning. I accidentally skipped it, so I've come back out especially.'

Both men are impressed by his commitment to duty. So much so the first ranger shares with Oyster Boy that he has in fact written to the council on several other matters in need of urgent attention, but he never hears back. And he wonders if he would be prepared to chase up these matters with the appropriate official on his behalf.

'Sure' he replies, 'be happy to.'

Which is how he ends up sitting by the side of a lake at night with two forest rangers, listening to their grievances and taking down notes beneath the light of their hats so that he might be fully prepared for a future conversation he would never have. They then say goodbye and Oyster Boy toddles off with his prize tucked beneath his arm. In my mind, he whistles as he goes, but he flat denies this, and I'd hate to stray into hyperbole.

By the time we finished lunch it was late into the afternoon, and I headed back to the hotel to recharge my batteries. I was asleep within seconds of cheek meeting pillow. I've suffered from insomnia most of my adult life. Turns out a ten-mile walk, plenty of beer, wine and whisky, and a good meal is the cure I was looking for. I must remember to tell my doctor. He might want to write a paper or something.

Later on we met up at the Love Café to watch some comedy. We continued drinking, though not particularly quickly or excessively. The evening had a low-profile feel to it after the day's exertions. Despite this, I began to feel a little worse for wear. As the last act finished, I bade the chaps goodnight and headed back to the hotel, which was only a fifteen-minute walk away.

After a few minutes, I realised I was going in the wrong direction. The obvious thing to do was turn around. But alcohol can fuel the imagination in strange ways. I decided that a good walk and some fresh air would help sober me up. So I continued to go the wrong way. My plan – which was vague at best – was to loop around at some point and circle back to the hotel from the opposite direction. As plans go, this was probably as stupid as any hatched by anyone, ever.

Two hours later I was still walking and totally lost. I tried Google Maps but couldn't get it together. That could have been down to bad service but was more likely idiot user.

I thought back to my impatience with the hapless cab driver earlier in the day.

Maybe this was the universe repaying me. Then, on an

otherwise deserted road, I saw a man sitting alone in a parked car. I thought it a little weird at that hour, but desperation was kicking in. I knocked on his window.

He looked up at me with some suspicion. I can't say I blame him. But he wound down the window a few inches.

'I'm sorry to bother you but I'm lost. Would you drive me back to my hotel for fifty pounds?'

'No.'

'A hundred?'

'Fuck off.'

And up the window went. There was nothing to be done but re-saddle Shanks's pony and press on.

Cold and tired, I eventually found my way back to the hotel at around 1.30 a.m. The wave of relief I felt quickly subsided as I found myself locked out. Peering through the glass, I could see no one on reception. I tried the doorbell. Nothing. I tried again. Still nothing.

Fuckety fucking fuck.

What is the point of running a hotel if you're not going to let people in? The entire hotel business model relies on you being inside of them. And half past one is hardly the witching hour. What happened to hip and happening 'Shoreditch on Sea'? Crash out early after a mug of cocoa, did it?

Out of energy, down on my luck, and low on inspiration, I did what many men before me have done for time immemorial. I turned to a woman for help. In this case my friend Jacky. The good sense I lack on occasions she has in abundance. She is considered, prepared and resourceful. M to my 007 license to stupid. I phoned and thankfully she picked up.

'I've had too much to drink and I'm locked out of my hotel. I think I may have to sleep on the beach. I don't want to sleep on the beach.'

'Have you tried calling them?'

'No.'

'Why not?

A few seconds' silence. 'I don't know.'

'Well, phone them.'

'I don't have the number.'

Ever patient, she asked me the name of the hotel and I told her. She texted me their details. I thanked her, hung up and called the hotel. It rang out several times before a woman answered. I again explained the situation, this time trying my best not to sound like I'd spent most of the day drinking.

Within a few minutes, she appeared and opened the door in her dressing gown. Why she had a door in her dressing gown, I cannot say. Her demeanour could not have been more frosty if she had a carrot for a nose.

'We do have an entry code, you know,' she snapped.

'No, I did not know,' I replied. 'Might I suggest you tell your guests about it *before* they go out?'

She said nothing, turned around and walked away. 'Goodnight,' I called.

Nisht.

I took the lift, walked to my room and swiped my card in the lock. The light stayed red. I tried again and again and again, hoping to hear that *click* that would let me know all was right in the world. There was no *click*.

So I phoned her again. My genie in a dressing gown appeared for a second time. If looks could kill, I'd have been a few hours off rigor mortis setting in. She produced her own card, which worked first time. Of course it fucking did.

I wanted to point out that none of this was my fault. But the problem with having been drinking is that it makes you look wrong even when you're in the right. So I maintained a diplomatic silence and went to bed. Thankfully, I'd never have to see her again.

In the morning as I went to leave, she was sitting on reception. So I made my exit with great stealth. Walking briskly with head down. Which, of course, is how my story began, and so would seem a suitable beat to end on.

EVERY TIME I SEE
A BLACK MAN IN A KILT,
I THINK OF HIM

I was hopping around channels looking for something to watch when I came across the Italian movie *Cinema Paradiso*. There's a handful of films I find hard to pass by, no matter how many times I've seen them. *Duck Soup*, *The Philadelphia Story*, *Annie Hall*, *Godfathers I* and *II*, *Jaws*, *The Silence of the Lambs*, *The Shawshank Redemption*, *Pretty Woman*, *Happy Gilmore*, and almost anything by Pedro Almodóvar. I must have seen some of them twenty or thirty times. *Cinema Paradiso* is also on the list, and if you're looking for a common denominator between that lot, it's probably that I suffer from multiple personality disorder.

The first time I saw *Cinema Paradiso* was with my wife-to-be back in the late eighties. It is a charming film and we both came away suitably charmed. We went for hot chocolate after and sat there talking about different aspects of the movie. We used to do that kind of thing back then.

Sadly our relationship would run into problems midway through a tricky second act and the story had an unhappy ending. One of the things I like about writing is that you can make life as it should be, rather than how it inevitably is. If that sounds a little mawkish, shoot me. I've always been partial to a spot of mawk. And while *Cinema Paradiso* stirs up some mixed emotions, it is still a movie I have a lot of time for. Not as much as I used to, obviously, because the ex-wife got half.

Written and directed by Giuseppe Tornatore, it's a coming-of-age yarn woven around the young protagonist Salvatore's burgeoning love of film under the tutelage of Alfredo, a kindly projectionist played by the marvellous Philippe Noiret. The story, which is told in flashback, is set just after World War II in the kind of picturesque Sicilian village you spend all day trying to find on holiday only to end up getting trampled to death by a battalion of Japanese tourists.

Cinema Paradiso is the name of the town's movie house. A few years before the introduction of TV, it is the hub of the local community. All life flows through its doors. The thing about the cinema – or picture house, as my nan insisted on calling it – being a part of the community struck a chord.

The locale I grew up in had little of the charm of Giancaldo, the village in the film. But we did have two cinemas, both situated nearby at Clapton Pond, separated only and somewhat bizarrely, by a church. The ABC, formerly known as the Ritz and the smaller, scruffier Kenning Hall – known to its patrons as 'the shithole' for reasons well merited. Once your feet hit the floor in that gaff, you were lucky to ever see them again.

My earliest recollection was the Saturday morning kids' club at the ABC. No adults, save for one poor sod armed with only a flashlight and 1,800 overexcited kids going batshit crazy. And yes it really was that busy. With no ball pits, laser tag or

World of Warcraft to keep youngsters occupied, it provided a rare opportunity for parents to grab a much-needed slice of peace and quiet. If they were told it was full and their kids couldn't come in, you'd see grown men fall to their knees and break down in tears.

'Please. I have money. There's only two of 'em. The little one's got polio.'

For those lucky enough to gain admittance, proceedings would commence with a rousing chorus of the ABC Minors Song:

> *We are the boys and girls well known as*
> *Minors of the ABC.*
> *And every Saturday all line up*
> *To see the films we like and shout aloud with glee.*
> *We like to laugh and have a sing-song*
> *Just a happy crowd are we.*
> *We're all pals together*
> *We're Minors of the ABC.*

If that makes it all sound like squeaky-clean fun, it belies the absolute anarchy that would follow. Kids would be rolling around on the floor tearing lumps off each other, jumping up and down on seats, lobbing handfuls of sweets high into the air and watching as they descended to carpet bomb the occupants of the rows below. It was glorious.

On-screen entertainment would begin with cartoons. Popeye, which I liked because he was a sailor who beat up bullies, and Mickey Mouse, which I didn't because he was an anodyne rodent wanker in bad clothes.

Next came the heroes. The Lone Ranger or, better still, Captain Marvel or Batman.

The Captain was a singularly unimpressive-looking bloke

in woollen tights and a cape. Batman was the same but with a naff mask thrown in. Could well have been the same geezer. It was impossible to hear the dialogue above the racket going on around you, but it didn't matter. No one gave a monkey's about plot development. It was all about watching the bad guys get what was coming to them and every blow landed would be met with a loud cheer.

With the villains defeated, the hero would make a short speech about justice prevailing and then shoot home to rinse out his tights in time for next week's adventure.

During the school holidays, my nan would round up all the kids and treat us to a matinee performance. On such occasions, there was no money to be wasted on popcorn or sweets. But we did not go hungry. About twenty minutes into the screening, she'd reach deep into her bag and pull out a whole roast chicken. She'd rip it up with her bare hands and pass the various body parts along the row to us. You have never truly experienced the magic of cinema until you've watched Chitty Chitty Bang Bang while gnawing on a greasy drumstick. And there was more. Hard-boiled eggs, which she'd crack on the back of the seat in front and then sit there shelling. And let's not forget the epitome of cinema snacks, the crab paste Wonderloaf sandwich. Today when I'm sitting trying to watch a film, cursing under my breath at the people in front, who appear to be eating a three-course meal purchased in the foyer, I cannot help but wonder if it wasn't my nan who inspired that business model.

Once a month on a Friday evening I would go to the pictures with my dad. The old man was a cabbie at the time and worked a lot of nights. So I never saw that much of him. I loved our 'boys' nights out'. I can't remember much about the films we saw, but I do recall the time a man a few rows in front stood up and started screaming angrily in a foreign language. He then got his dick out and started waving it around.

'Dad, look.'

'Take no notice, son.'

Easier said than done, father. I was horrified but all around us people followed my old man's sage advice and pretended it wasn't happening. In the end, he tired himself out, zipped up and sat down again. The cinema staff had done nothing throughout. They'd just let him get on with it. Well, it was the Kenning Hall. Anything less than a rape and triple homicide probably constituted a quiet night for them.

By my early teenage years, I was too caught up in music and clothes to be bothered with film. Trailing in, in a poor third place, were girls, who I was also beginning to notice.

Myself and the chaps did go to see *Bronco Bullfrog*, a small British film that supposedly embraced suedehead culture. It was set in Stratford and featured a cast of mainly young non-actors. This was a ploy way ahead of its time, but we weren't impressed. It was a kitchen-sink drama and had about as much to do with suedeheads as Henry Kissinger. But kudos to the kitchen sink, which was way more charismatic than the cast.

A few months after this, my friends and I were out one day, strolling around and about. Strolling around and about was a much-favoured pastime amongst the chaps, partly on account of us having nowhere else pressing to be but also because it allowed us to see and be seen.

On this occasion, we were seen by a man who claimed to be a casting director and said he wanted to put us in a film. A quickly arrived at consensus decided he was a nonce and he was given short shrift. Nonces not being the kind of personage deserving of normal-length shrift. But he was persistent and persuasive. He produced a business card. And in fairness, it did say casting director, and not nonce. I was convinced and my esteemed colleagues followed suit. He asked if we knew any other kids like us. Was he serious? We only knew kids like us. The call went out and the few became many. The lessons of *Bronco Bullfrog* were all but forgotten. The combined skinhead forces of Hackney, Stamford Hill and Chingford were about to be in the movies.

Made, a film directed by John Mackenzie, featuring *Poor Cow* actress Carol White and musician Roy Harper, was eventually released in 1972. It told the depressing story of a depressed woman who led a depressing life. I watched it once and retrospectively would have to say I've had more enjoyable colonoscopies. White's character was Valerie, who was a single parent, probably because it made her lot even more miserable. The film's big scene was a knock-off from *Battleship Potemkin*, where a pram with her baby in it goes crashing down a steep flight of stairs, killing the baby. How did such a terrible accident come to pass? Mother and child were out taking a walk and minding their own business when they happen to pass by a football ground and get caught up in a riot started by hooligans. And that is where we came in.

We were taken to Stamford Bridge on a match day, where base had been set up outside the ground. The director talked us through what he wanted us to do and then produced a crate of bottles made from harmless sugar glass. He explained what they were and warned us they were expensive and in short supply and only to be used on his command. A lunatic called Ian Hastie, who I went to school with, immediately picked one up and smashed it over his head. It was very funny and set the tone for what would follow.

Wardrobe gave us red-and-white football scarves to wear. A bunch of professional extras were given the same in blue and white. These would be the two rival gangs. On

Mackenzie's word, we had to charge them and a mock fight would ensue.

The extras, who considered themselves real actors, were not at all thrilled about our involvement and had been sniffy towards us all day. So with the benefit of hindsight, dividing us neatly into two opposing factions may not have been the smartest move in the world.

Even dumber was waiting until the game was over and the crowd had begun to surge out onto the street before shouting 'action'. On cue, we charged. The altercation that followed quickly escalated from overly enthusiastic to borderline bundle. We went the full Lee Strasberg on their asses.

Either by accident or design, Chelsea happened to be playing Arsenal that day. As the real supporters leaving the ground were confronted by a mass brawl between red and blue, they piled in. At which point shit got seriously real. Ten quid cash in hand and a free lunch was not enough to go up against the Shed, and I quietly extricated myself from the surrounding chaos and bid them all an Irish goodbye.

Most of this ended up on the cutting-room floor. But there was a great close-up shot of Ginger Richard from Stamford Hill in his black Harrington and Fred Perry shouting, 'Get the bastards!' He dined out on that at the Stamford Hill Wimpy Bar for years to come.

In the film, Roy Harper played – surprise, surprise – a musician who had a brief fling with Valerie and then wrote a song about the various tragedies that made up her shit show of a life. In an unlikely turn of events, Harper's path would again cross my own some years later in a way that did me a lot more good than he ever did poor old Val. By 1978, while still a musician, he was doubling up as a gentleman farmer. It was the kind of thing hippies did back then. One fateful day one of his sheep got sick and its heart stopped beating. Roy leapt into action and gave the poor creature the kiss of life. It lived but repaid its saviour by giving him a nasty dose of sheep AIDS or whatever it is you catch from kissing sheep.

None of which would mean much to anyone outside of the Harper family if he hadn't been booked to record a session for John Peel the following day. Peel's producer, John Walters, rang up, related the sorry tale and asked if the Buzzards would be available to take his place. This was the first instance of a hand being physically bitten off down a phone line in the history of telecommunications.

It would be the first of several sessions we recorded at the BBC studios in Maida Vale for Peel. You'll no doubt have heard many bands praise the late DJ for the invaluable support he gave their careers. You can add me to the list. In those halcyon days of new bands, indie labels and small gigs, he was the linchpin that made it all work. Exposure on his show fuelled the scene. The man's contribution to music and culture was nothing short of immense.

Even before that, film continued to play second fiddle to music in my life, though it did get a boost of kinds when I began dating in earnest. When you were too young to get into pubs, the cinema was one of the few places you could take a girl for a night out. With the added bonus of potential back-row shenanigans after the lights went down. Hands slowly edging up skirts. Pushed away just as things were getting interesting. But gently, so as not to entirely discourage you. A minute later you'd try again, hoping the kissing marathon you were now both immersed in would distract her long enough to make further progress. This dance would continue for the endurance in cinemas all over the country. As the film came to an end, lines of young men could be seen limping uncomfortably towards the exit.

My friend Tony Islin, who had a regular girlfriend,

persuaded me to go on a double date with them and one of her friends, whom I'd never met. I wasn't a big fan of the whole blind-date scenario but when a mate's trying to score some brownie points with his missus, what kind of friend would you be not to lend a helping hand?

We met outside the Stamford Hill Odeon and I quickly wished I'd been the kind of friend who'd told his mate to fuck off. My 'date' looked ten years older than me. Which to a sixteen-year-old made her a potential candidate for mummification. She wore a black polo neck, large-framed glasses, and her long dark hair was worn up. And her name was Hilary. What kind of name was Hilary?

To make matters worse, her disappointment at seeing me was so palpable it made me feel like the keen one. The disdain sprayed from her pores in my direction. This did not stop Hilary from standing back with Tony's girlfriend when it came to paying for admission. I coughed up. She did not deign to thank me. I sensed there would be no hand slowly edging its way up a skirt tonight. Hilary probably had a bear trap set there anyway.

The film was *Love Story*, a huge box-office hit that year about a man whose girlfriend dies of leukaemia. Lucky him, I sat there thinking. Of course, I should have settled back, watched the movie and chalked it up to experience. It wasn't like Hilary was elbowing me in the kidneys or anything. Hilary was taciturn. Which confused me, as I didn't know what the word meant. But halfway through I excused myself, saying I was going to the bathroom and did a runner. Didn't stop moving till I hit Seven Sisters Road. Adieu, sweet Hilary.

Tony was pissed off with me and later demanded an apology. I told him love means never having to say you're sorry.

That aside, the seventies saw a slew of great movies. *A Clockwork Orange, Alien, Get Carter, Enter the Dragon, Rocky,*

Chinatown, One Flew Over the Cuckoo's Nest, Taxi Driver, The French Connection, Carrie, The Exorcist, the first two *Godfathers,* and the wonderful *Harold and Maude.*

Sitting in the dark and getting lost in these worlds and stories became an essential part of my week. If no one I knew wanted to see something that interested me, I would happily go alone. I think I actually preferred that. Back-row shenanigans went out of the window. These films demanded your full attention, and the lure of the vagina was at least partially eclipsed. Especially after watching *The Exorcist.* I couldn't go near one for months after that.

As if by magic, these giant slabs of wonder would appear fully formed in my local cinema. It never occurred to me that there were vision, art and great craft in play. All I could see were the results. When I look back at the pre-internet, pre-hundreds-of-TV-channels days of my youth, I'm struck by both how much we did and how little we knew. About anything, really.

The man responsible for first opening my eyes was Barry Norman, who hosted the annual *Film* series on the BBC. Bazza was more like a nice uncle than the kind of film critic we are used to today. Though it's true to say not like any uncle I had, as mine were all cockneys in overcoats who drove black cabs. He had a friendly middle-class demeanour and a love of film. I sat glued to the screen as he talked us through that week's new releases and from time to time interviewed a famous actor or director. He was knowledgeable and witty and always made me want to know more. It would have been nice to have had a few teachers at school like that, but as my late mother used to say, 'If ifs and ands were pots and pans, there'd be no work for tinkers' hands.' She had an impressive collection of aphorisms, my old woman. Would have been worth a fortune at today's prices.

A little knowledge being a dangerous thing wasn't one

of her favourites, but it was becoming true of me and film. I was mad about *Jaws*. Went to see it again and again. No great surprise there. It was the highest-grossing movie of its time and the first-ever summer blockbuster. At some point it began to dawn on me that it was not really a movie about a man-eating great white shark at all. It was about three very different men locked together in a life-or-death situation. How they reacted and interacted, how they each measured up to the challenge, was the heart of the movie. We hardly saw the shark. But the tension and expectation, heightened by John Williams' genius tuba motif, were so effective we didn't even notice. This blew my mind.

I could not wait to share these revelations with friends who had also seen the film. The response *en masse* was, 'Fuck off, you prick. Of course it's about a man-eating shark. It's called *Jaws*, isn't it?'

In later years I would learn that the ground-breaking – and ground-breakingly expensive – animatronic sharks Spielberg had made for *Jaws* refused to function properly in salt water. So he had been forced to think creatively. Happy accident or not, it was the first time I looked inside a movie and saw a little of what made it tick.

I have always been clumsy with my hands. I cannot fix things and have no concept of how they work. I can't even draw, which frustrates me endlessly. My friend Liz once invited me along to see her pose for a life-drawing class and to try my hand. I enjoyed the event. There was music and old black-and-white film was projected behind her as she worked. She was amazing. Unabashed, obviously. But equally happy to hold unflattering, uncomfortable poses for long periods as those which made her look more traditionally beautiful. Never underestimate other people's skills.

All around me, others in the class were busy sketching

away with pencils and charcoal. I kept peeking and within minutes I could see interesting interpretations of Liz doing her stuff start to take shape. Meanwhile, I spent all night stuck on one tit that I was unable to get right. Which was ironic because it was her right tit. At the end of the session, as our work was presented, I slipped down, embarrassed, in my chair. Mine looked like a grey, knotted condom full of water floating alone in the cosmos. Liz was very generous in her appraisal. But she knew her tit didn't look like that. We all did.

English aside, I'd been spectacularly average at school. Most of my energy had gone into trying to make my classmates laugh. Conventional wisdom suggests that such behaviour tends to be an escape route from bullying. Not so in my case. I would punch kids that didn't think I was funny.

Understanding films, albeit at an elementary level, was one of the first things I ever felt vaguely good at. And that made me feel good about myself. For less than a quid, I could have a good night out and get my esteem boosted. Value for money indeed.

I'm going to blame punk for bringing this period of auto-didactic growth to an abrupt end. Once I started a band, I was simply too busy rehearsing, touring and recording for much else.

Except it isn't true. You can always find time for the things you really want to do. But when I'm excited by something, it tends to be all-consuming. I don't have the moderate gene. I'm more foot to the floor in one direction. This has its advantages. I'm focused, driven and can work insane hours. But there's a downside. While immersed in my latest obsession, other things get neglected. The truth is, film simply wasn't sparkly enough to command my attention at that point in my life. And it would stay that way through the Leyton Buzzards, Modern Romance and my time working with Divine.

In 1987 I briefly started a third band. I'd seen the Beastie Boys in New York and they'd blown me away. In the UK Mick Jones's Big Audio Dynamite and Tony James's Sigue Sigue Sputnik were both pursuing exciting new directions, and it was very much off that combined energy that USSA – as we were known – was created.

The core of the band was me, Paul Gendler and Laurie Wisefield. Paul had been in Modern Romance and personality-wise was like Larry David with postnatal depression.

Happiness was not in his repertoire. But he was a brilliant funk rhythm guitarist – for my money, up there with Nile Rodgers – and a mate. Laurie had been in Wishbone Ash and was a top-drawer rock lead guitarist. We'd met because he was living with a friend of mine, Sally, who was the girl shaking her booty on the cover of 'Saturday Night Beneath the Plastic Palm Trees'. I'd never worked with two guitarists before and thought putting them together could be a phenomenal combination. And it was. Our sound was a mash-up of rock, funk, punk, pop and rap. I loved it.

We wrote and recorded close to an album. Our songs had titles like 'The Day the Mafiosa Fought the Three-Course War', 'Back in the USSA' and 'Johnny Cee Fax'. Which in themselves merited a record contract. We had some great pictures taken and then played a showcase gig for record companies in town.

We got offered a deal off the back of that. Nothing great, just a couple of singles. But I wasn't bothered. I knew 'Mafiosa' was a slam-dunk hit and after that, we'd be on our way.

And yet you haven't heard of USSA or the tune in question. Don't feel embarrassed.

It's a club most of the world belongs to. So what happened?

Mainly what happened was Laurie got a call from Tina Turner asking him to be her lead guitarist. Faced with a choice of Geoffbeans or the sort in the syrup who can sing a bit, he very sensibly opted for the latter. And who can blame him?

Laurie was integral to the band's sound, so that left me in a bit of a two and eight. As I was trying to figure it out, Paul announced that he'd been offered a tour playing with Level 42 and he too was on his bike. Maybe it was my choice of cologne? Anyway, that was the end of that. With barely a whimper, let alone a bang.

Being an impulsive sort with a tendency to jump in first and ask questions later, I don't have too many 'what ifs' amongst my emotional baggage. I'm more of a 'why the fuck did I do that?' kind of guy. USSA was the exception. It wasn't about money or, God forbid, fame, which I have below zero interest in. Or even the missed chance of being in a band with two mates again. But never knowing how your work would have been received? That was the bastard gift that kept on giving.

I didn't blame either of them for their choices. But I'd wasted a year of my life and my funds were so exhausted they needed a lie-down. I was done with bands. Now I needed to work out what to do next.

I've always been a big fan of TV comedy, sitcoms especially. I'd been a little too young to fully appreciate classics like *Steptoe and Son* and *The Likely Lads*, but I'd always enjoyed John Sullivan's *Just Good Friends* and *Only Fools and Horses*, and like everyone else had found *Fawlty Towers* hilarious. My favourite show was *Porridge*, starring Ronnie Barker as imprisoned career criminal Norman Stanley Fletcher, written by Dick Clement and Ian La Frenais. The writing was beautiful and Barker's pitch-perfect performance a masterclass in comedic acting.

In the mid-eighties Friday night was US comedy night on Channel 4. This was a golden age of American sitcoms, and one show, more than any other, showed the genre at its most impressive: *Cheers*, the Boston basement bar where everybody knew your name. For my money, the greatest sitcom ever produced. I cannot overstate the effect watching that pilot episode had on me. It was up there with hearing Roxy's debut album or 'Anarchy in the UK' for the first time. All instantly creating new neuropathways in my nut that would remain intact for a lifetime.

Why was *Cheers* so much more impactful on me than its British counterparts? On a fundamental level, it's smarter, sharper and quicker. But I think there's more to it than that.

Broadly speaking, our homegrown comedies tend to be about losers, idiots or terminal fuck-ups. Or any combination thereof. This can be very funny. But culturally it's not something I connect with. Emotions are kept in check and often shrouded in cynicism. Again, it provides plenty of laughs, but as an emotionally demonstrative person from a long line of people who find it physically impossible not to express every single thing they ever feel, it's a little like watching an alien life form. I get it but I don't feel it. The Brits also have a penchant for vulgarity, which you can trace back to music hall, saucy seaside postcards and probably Chaucer. There, I have to admit I'm somewhat patriotic. I've always had a soft spot for a knob gag. Or maybe it's a hard spot?

See what I did there?

Even though its setting was ostensibly blue-collar, the comedy of *Cheers* was remarkably sophisticated. Its roots were in earlier great American shows like *Taxi* – which I loved – but also the plays of Neil Simon and the films of Hepburn and Tracy and the Marx Brothers. If the Algonquin round table had watched *Cheers* on their little get-togethers, I have no doubt you'd have heard the likes of Dorothy Parker and George S. Kaufman roaring with laughter.

What we think of as American comedy is in truth a derivative of Jewish comedy. As such, it speaks to me loud and clear. Despite the fact I'm such a rubbish Jew my sons aren't circumcised and my bar mitzvah fell on Xmas Eve.

The eighties were the time of the VCR recorder. I had hundreds of hours of US comedy recorded on cassette. *Cheers*, *The Golden Girls* and *Roseanne*, to name but a few. All were neatly labelled and organised as only a true obsessive would. I never recorded over anything. That would have been like book burning.

With time on my hands, I began working my way through my video library. Not with any thoughts of a new career in mind. I just wanted to watch them all. The thrill American movies had given me in the seventies, American sitcoms gave me in the eighties.

After a while, a pattern began to emerge. I reached for a pen and paper and began taking notes. Soon I was deconstructing them. I'd done something similar when teaching myself how to write songs. And would do so again when I got into writing screenplays. The great thing about being a consummate fanboy is that the very best is all out there for you to learn from. Fuck creative writing courses when you can watch *Cheers* or *The Sopranos*.

As US sitcoms are delivered in large quantities, they are written by teams headed up by a showrunner, who is invariably also a former writer. It's a slick set-up and the results are pleasingly consistent and surprisingly uniform. Which means they are quite straightforward to break down. 'A' plots, 'B' plots, acts and structure and characters, those little writerly tricks that keep cropping up again and again. I ended up with a ten-page template on how to write a sitcom.

All that remained was to give it a test run. I will not burden you with the concept I came up with for my first-ever script. It was cheesier than a fondue buffet at a Swiss orgy. Having said that, it did not prevent one of the production companies it was sent to – who turned it down – from coming up with a stunningly similar idea the following year and getting it commissioned.

Concept aside, I was pleased with the results. It moved along quickly and all the right things happened in the right places. And it had three good laughs a page. Which looked to be the benchmark of the shows I was seeking to emulate.

There was one small problem. All my characters sounded American. Not surprising, given the intensity and provenance of my tuition programme.

Pushing that concern to one side, I sent it off to a bunch of agents. One responded quickly. We met for a coffee and a chat, after which she took me on as a client. I didn't give any real consideration to the implications of this career shift. In my mind, I was still making shit up with the intention of presenting it for public consumption. Only this way I wouldn't be reliant on other musicians. Underthinking things has always been one of my greatest virtues.

My new agent arranged for me to meet Alomo Productions. They were a hugely successful comedy-based company with hit shows like *Birds of a Feather*, *Goodnight Sweetheart* and *The New Statesman* under their belt. A week later I found myself in a room with their prolific creators Laurence Marks and Maurice Gran – known to all as 'Lo and Mo'. They couldn't have been nicer. Though Laurence clearly hailed from a far-off galaxy and would only visit earth from time to time, Maurice was a friendly, funny Jewish bloke with an air of the naughty schoolboy about him. Also present was the late Allan McKeown, a producer who was partners with *Porridge* writers Clement and La Frenais and whose company owned Alomo.

McKeown was one of those characters that fascinate people like me. He'd been a hairdresser from Hainault who'd worked on various TV shows, as well as films such as *Get Carter*. Deciding there was more fun and money to be had from showbusiness than doing people's barnets, he became a producer instead. This was the sixties. You could do things like that back then.

He went on to make many shows, such as the brilliant *Auf Wiedersehen, Pet* in the UK, as well as producing for all the major US networks. In his spare time, he married Tracey Ullman and became a multi-millionaire.

Months after our first introduction, I was in a writer's meeting at Alomo's offices when Allan burst in without knocking. Which is fair enough, seeing as he owned the gaff. He pointed at me and said, 'Geoff Deane. Pitching a new idea for Tracey to CBS in LA. I want you with me and to write the show. You on board?'

Was I on board? I was already packed, mate. I went home and told the missus and we spent the evening imagining our new life in LA. Naturally not another word about the show was ever mentioned again. Which was very Allan. But he was such a charming and entertaining ball of energy, it was quite impossible to dislike the man. He was also a great storyteller. As you may have heard, I'm quite partial to a story myself, so I was always an enthusiastic listener.

Here's one that stayed in my mind. After first making his money, Allan treated himself to a vintage Rolls-Royce. Keen to do things properly, he also hired a man to maintain the vehicle. After a while, Allan found that whenever he asked to use the car, it was invariably 'in the shop' having some work done. So much so that he began to doubt the wisdom of his very expensive purchase. But his man explained that it was quite normal for such a classic car to require regular fine-tuning.

On one occasion when the Roller was on the road, Allan dropped his keys on the floor after removing them from the ignition. Bending down to pick them up, he noticed some tiny shreds of paper beneath the driver's seat. He retrieved one on his fingertip. Confetti. A little amateur-detective work later, Allan discovered that the bloke had been running a side hustle hiring his cherished motor out for weddings. It was the notion of Allan being out-Allaned that I found most amusing.

I came away from that first meeting with a commission to write an episode of *Birds of a Feather*. I'd only been a writer for about fifteen minutes and this was a hit TV show.

Result.

No one seemed bothered that my script, which they had all liked, was 'American'. They just assumed I could do the same in 'English'. Figuring I'd better learn sharpish, I watched episodes of *Porridge* around the clock before starting to write.

Birds, as you no doubt know, is about two sisters, Sharon and Tracey (Pauline Quirke and Linda Robson), whose partners are in prison. And of course their next-door neighbour Dorien Green (Lesley Joseph). She's married but we never see her husband. Neither did she, come to think of it.

When I looked at the show, I saw three women without men. So I approached it something like an English *Golden Girls*, while cranking all the characters up a notch. Bigger, brighter, bolder. And the East End/Essex setting was a gift.

I wanted my first episode to land with a bang, so I pulled out all the stops. Which in this instance entailed writing a set piece for Dorien where she sang and performed Madonna's 'Like a Virgin'. Lesley's a real old-school trouper and a fantastic comic actor. She really knocked it out of the park. At one point while singing, she lay on her back and began opening and closing her legs in the air to the beat. The audience lapped it up.

After the recording, Laurence said to me that it had been a perfect episode of the show. I'd worn out the carpet in the control room pacing up and down during the recording. So that was good to hear.

The show got great feedback from the public and the BBC ran that clip of Lesley again and again. I decided I might stick with this comedy-writing business for a bit.

Birds picked up a fair bit of flak from critics over the years, which I think was harsh.

The show could be uneven. But that was because Lo and Mo were trying to introduce the American-style team-writing system. That's how I got my break. There wasn't the infrastructure in place, or perhaps the depth of writing talent they had in the US, to achieve the same level of consistency. But when it worked, it was a very funny show with a terrific cast. In 1993 I was lucky enough to be asked to write the Xmas special. The episode, 'It Happened in Hollywood', where the sisters try to track down the father they'd never known, pulled in almost 20 million viewers. So we must have been doing something right.

The shoot in Hollywood was great fun and went well. 'Gorgeous' George Hamilton joined the cast and he was a funny geezer. I saw him sunbathing with a tinfoil reflector aimed under his chin to ensure an even tan on his Gregory Peck. That went straight into the script.

On one occasion I went out clothes shopping with Lesley. In an upmarket boutique, she decided to try on a pair of skinny jeans. Being an actor and used to getting her kit on and off, she didn't bother using the changing room and just slipped behind a clothes rail. She squeezed herself into the jeans, which looked like they'd been sprayed on, but Lesley was in good shape and could carry them off. She asked me what I thought and I gave her the thumbs-up. At which point, still on semi-public display, she pulled the jeans down.

Unfortunately, as they were so tight, everything she had on beneath came down with them. And suddenly there was a growler loose on Rodeo Drive. The super-camp store manager said, 'Oh my God,' and quietly slipped into a coma. Lesley didn't seem much bothered and calmly pulled it all up again. I considered putting that in the script too, but what with the show going out after people had just had their Xmas lunch, I decided it might not be appropriate.

I rounded off the American trip by getting married around a swimming pool in Hollywood. You can take the boy out of the band and all that. Lesley, Linda and Pauline were brides-maids, so any chance of it being an emotional occasion went right out the window. I also wore a truly ghastly Versace shirt, which would later be cited as grounds for divorce.

My years working with Lo and Mo would count among some of the most pleasurable of my professional life. Sitting around a table with a bunch of funny people throwing ideas around, all trying to make each other laugh, was not a bad way to earn a living. And I became great friends with some of the other writers. Gary Lawson, John Phelps, former stand-up Jenny Lecoat and the late Paul Makin. I loved Paul. Both bonkers and a genius, he was one of the funniest human beings I have ever met.

I was also very fond of the writer and actor Danny Peacock, who for a time was developing some projects with the company. We even worked together for a bit. When I first met Danny, he was depressed and in a bad place. His girlfriend, Amanda Holden, had dumped him for the comedian Les Dennis and he had taken it very badly. That her new relationship was in the tabloids every other day did nothing to help matters.

A few months later Danny rang me and he sounded much brighter. Joyful, in fact. He told me he'd been walking through Soho the previous night and as he turned into Old Compton Street he'd seen Les Dennis lying on the pavement, paralytically drunk. Danny stood over him, raised both arms in the air and treated him to a rousing chorus of 'There's only one Danny Peacock' before walking off triumphantly. Closure by any other name.

The most important friendship I made during this period was with Mia Jupp, who had started at Alomo as a runner and worked her way up to line producer. She was a no-nonsense, smart, hard-grafting, working-class girl whom the crew adored. We hit it off immediately and became mates and colleagues for life. When I formed my own production company, she came with me and eventually became an award-winning producer. She was some woman, Mia.

In 2021 we were still working together. This time on a project with crime author Kimberley Chambers. Covid had kicked in and we were doing our meetings via Zoom. I noticed Mia had lost a bit of weight and she said she hadn't been feeling too good. She'd tested negative but was going to the hospital for some tests. It was just four months later that I was walking through Stansted Airport, having returned from visiting my boy Woody in Lisbon, when her husband Mat's name flashed up on my phone. I answered it. 'She's gone, mate,' he said quietly. I felt like the world had fallen off its axis.

I was sitting with both of my parents when they took their last breaths. I've also lost good mates. It's the downside of getting older and, well, not having kicked the bucket yourself. But Mia's death left me heartbroken. It was all kinds of wrong in all kinds of ways. That she left a husband and three young sons just added to the sheer rotten fuckery of it all.

I was honoured to be asked to say a few words at her funeral. It wasn't a great performance. I had a lump in my throat the size of the Rosetta Stone and I couldn't hold back the tears. But it gave me a chance to say goodbye and I also got a few laughs. I think my dear friend would have approved.

After I exited Modern Romance, *The Face* magazine had asked me to do some record reviews for them. They'd been received well and I began to contribute fairly regularly.

Funny, day-in-the-life-of kind of stuff. Jonathan Ross's producer read one of them and asked me in for a chat. After which I began to write the occasional monologue for Jonathan on his chat show.

I liked Jonathan. He was a working-class Londoner, funny and a massive enthusiast. Like a better version of myself. Or worse. Depending on how you look at it. I never thought Jonathan needed writers. He was quite capable of talking to camera for five minutes and getting laughs without my help. But I kept that to myself.

I enjoyed working with other people on their shows more than you might expect. Unlike Marks and Gran, who seemed to come up with great ideas in their sleep, I found originating new concepts hard work. I was very self-critical and perfected a routine of developing, reworking and tweaking them over a period of many months before finally throwing them in the sea, where they undoubtedly belonged.

Writing for Jonathan, or *Birds* or *Chef* or whatever, all I had to do was write for someone or something that already existed. It was relatively stress-free and there's a lot to be said for that.

I would eventually go on to write shows of my own, but first I had an unexpected detour as film re-entered my life. This time professionally, and way ahead of schedule.

I was told by my agent that Franc Roddam had asked to meet me. Franc was a name I was familiar with for two somewhat exemplary reasons. He was the man who came up with the idea for a show about British builders working in Germany, which Clement and La Frenais had spun so adeptly into *Auf Wiedersehen, Pet*. And he also directed the legendary mod movie *Quadrophenia*. With two headlines like that on his CV, I didn't need asking twice.

Now Franc was a very nice bloke. But it has to be said, by the time we met he had made his fortune and relocated to LA. Which has been known on occasions to impact on British sensibilities more than somewhat.

Franc told me that he had an idea for a film and he wanted me to write it.

I cannot tell you how excited I was to hear those words. My first movie. This was incredible. Fuck sitcoms, I was off to the Oscars, baby. At some point, I came down to earth long enough to ask him what the idea was.

At which point he got up and left his office.

He returned a few seconds later carrying a life-sized cardboard cut-out, which he stood up in the centre of the room and pointed towards. It was a mock-up of Eddie Murphy wearing a kilt and full Scottish regalia. The first of several alarm bells went off in my head. As Franc explained his idea, I tried to keep an open mind, even though I could feel the drawbridge raised higher with every word. Eddie Murphy plays a streetwise New York hustler who by some hilarious miracle of genealogy finds he's the new head of a Scottish clan. And guess what? It was called *Clan*. I kid you not, motherfuckers. The bells got louder.

He compared it to *King Ralph*, a bog-standard American movie in which John Goodman's gauche Vegas lounge singer became the King of England and also the excellent *Fresh Prince of Bel-Air*, where a young Will Smith played a Philly street kid sent to live with rich relatives. Franc was right in as much as they were all fish-out-of-water comedies. The problem was, his fish was a black dude and the water was very, very white, albeit with a Scottish accent. Every gag would have racial undertones. If not overtones. *Clan* was a potential horror show of gigantic proportions.

I knew I had to turn it down. Better still, run for the hills and never look back. But when Franc asked me if I was in, I heard myself saying yes. I can't really explain or justify it. Other than the fact he was Franc Roddam and I desperately wanted to write a movie.

The actual writing was a nightmare. I avoided mining the central conflict the story was based on for the entire screenplay, thus completely eliminating the possibility of causing any offence. In doing so I also eliminated the possibility of there being any gags. There was not one in the entire script. Franc read it and called me in. He sat there stony-faced. Then he asked me bluntly why it was so unfunny. I could have said because I spent 120 pages tap dancing around racist landmines set by your fucking terrible idea, Franc. But that would have been like calling him an idiot. And besides, if I felt like that, why on earth had I taken the job on?

So I mumbled an apology.

And Franc promptly commissioned me to write a second draft.

I tried. I really did. But I couldn't hack it. Which is when I decided to make a bad situation even worse. I'd become friends with Jez Stephenson, one of Jonathan's regular writers. His style was very different from mine, but Jez was a talent and I always liked his work. So I commissioned him to write the screenplay that Franc had commissioned me to write. I would pass it off as my own and fulfil my side of the contract.

If Franc had liked Jez's version and made the film, that story would have made a much better movie than *Clan*. The film within a film would go on to be a huge success and Jez would end up killing me for basking in the glory that was rightly his. Or maybe I'd be taken out by anti-racists. Either way, I'd end up brown bread, which was probably no more than I deserved.

But Jez's take on *Clan* was just as bad as mine. Different but equally shithouse. It did not end well with Franc, and my big break into the movie business was flushed away down the shitter of disappointment.

Years later I bumped into Franc. I was a little higher up the food chain by then and still felt bad about my part in the *Clan* debacle. So I confessed all. I hoped with the passage of time Franc might see the funny side.

Did he, fuck.

I said I was sorry and that if there was ever anything I could ever do to make it up to him, he should just ask.

'You can give me the money back,' he said coldly. 'Anything apart from that?' I replied.

Franc turned and walked away. That was the last we ever saw of each other. But every time I see a black man in a kilt, I think of him.

NO BUSINESS LIKE
SHOE BUSINESS

In the late nineties, I pitched a sitcom to ITV. At that time their reputation for comedy was marginally less impressive than Hermann Göring's and they were out of the sitcom game altogether. So this was the longest of shots.

My genius – if flawed – notion was to present them with something bright and shiny but easily digestible. *Friends*, but with a chromosome or two of *On the Buses* – the last ITV sitcom I or anyone had liked – injected into its DNA. It worked. Well, to a degree. The show, *Babes in the Wood* was commissioned, ran for two series and a lot of people watched it.

To say it was not received well by critics would be putting it mildly. One in particular took it upon himself to decimate the show – and me as its creator – at every opportunity.

He'd write about it even when it hadn't been on telly. And he continued to take the piss out of it after it had been decommissioned and was off the air. Something I felt he was largely responsible for. It was unusual for a show with such healthy viewing figures to be consigned to the dumper.

To be fair, I hadn't expected good reviews. The show

had attracted a ludicrous amount of attention before it was ever shown. There was even an item on the news about it. I knew it could never live up to the hype. It wasn't the kind of thing critics would like anyway. I was aiming for the *Birds of a Feather* zone. The critics were never kind to *Birds*, but millions of people were always happy to watch it. That would do me nicely.

I'd previously run the gamut of journalistic appraisal with my bands the Leyton Buzzards and Modern Romance. The Buzzards were generally loved and received some glorious reviews. Modern Romance, which was way more successful, was regularly hauled over burning-hot coals and then ritually slaughtered for shits and giggles. It was all water off a duck's back. Morrissey once said, *'There are indeed worse groups than Modern Romance. But can anyone seriously think of one?'* I thought it was hilarious. No one repeated it more than I did. Being blasé – or its rather less likeable brother, cocky – comes easily when you're touring the world, on telly all the time, and earning a nice few quid.

The slating *Babes* received was a whole different ball game. For one thing, I was no longer getting the esteem boost provided by performing in front of enthused audiences every other night. I was a bloke trying to forge a new career for himself. And it wasn't the music press. This was daily newspapers. Now everyone could read what a prick I was.

To crank the pressure up, I'd recently started my own little production company and it was our first commission. It was important to us. When the show was eventually canned, I had to tell a lot of people I was very fond of that the gig was over. I never enjoyed being a boss. I wasn't cut from the right cloth. And that was as wretched as anything I've ever had to do.

A few months after that I was sitting in a members' bar in Soho talking to my friend Mia Jupp. I was trying to persuade her to come and work for me. Considering I'd just had my only show kicked into touch and her current employers, Lo and Mo, were the most successful comedy writers in the country, this was a long way from an offer she couldn't refuse.

We were deep in convo when a figure entered the bar. I recognised him immediately by his middle-class white-man dreadlocks. Which in themselves could merit a defence of justifiable homicide. It was the dude I blamed for taking down my show.

My pulse began to race. I could see Mia's lips moving but no longer heard a word she was saying.

'Would you excuse me for a minute, Mi?'

'Sure.'

I got up and walked over to him. He was enjoying a drink at the bar with his back towards me.

I am not proud of what happened next. For sure, it was not my finest hour. On the other hand, it would be disingenuous to say I regret it.

What did I do?

I kicked him up the arse. Right in the middle of the Groucho Club. He turned around more in shock than pain and looked at me. I never said a word. Didn't have to. He made a dash for the exit. I followed him. Kicking him up the arse some more along the way. He was out of the door in seconds and legging it up Dean Street.

I returned to Mia.

'Sorry about that. Where were we?'

'I definitely want to work for you,' was all she said. And lucky for me, she did.

Getting slagged off for writing a show that had been condemned as downmarket had another, fairly obvious impact on me. I resolved to 'write up' for my next project. Or to put it another way, I would show those fuckers what I was capable of.

I had written a lot of TV narrative comedy by then. I love sitcom as a genre but was growing tired of the constraints that then typified it. Everything shot in front of a studio audience. Annoying canned laughter. Self-contained storylines that restored the status quo at the end of every episode, week in, week out. It was time to try something different.

My next show was called *A Many Splintered Thing*. It was about Russell, a married man who was having an affair. I liked to think of him as an accidental adulterer. He was not the kind of bloke who had affairs and was thoroughly miserable at having become one. His wife was not the kind of woman any sane man would cheat on. She was beautiful and intelligent, loving and supportive. The girlfriend was not typical mistress material either. Funny, offbeat and undemanding. She was also, by the by, having an on-off lesbian affair with her boss Camilla, who would later become her stalker. Still with me? Finally, we had my favourite character, Russell's best friend and confidante Luis. As drag queen Talullah he was brash, vulgar and outspoken. As himself, quiet, shy and wracked with self-doubt. It was Luis, played by the excellent Victor McGuire, who deftly nailed the punchline to what I thought was the best joke of the series. Susanna, the wife, had begun to sense Russell was losing interest in her. She was something of a dry character and went to see Luis – who she usually had no time for – and asked him to teach her how to be more fun. He looked horrified at the prospect.

'I'm sorry, Susanna. I don't think I can. I wouldn't know how.'

'Of course you can. You're a fun person. You dress up as a woman. You sing and dance around on stage and tell outrageous jokes.'

'Yes, but I'm crying on the inside.'

Writing it was exciting. I tore up a lot of the rules I used to work by. Out went my minimum of three-gags-a-page mantra. If things became sad or serious, I would go with it. As long as it was good, it didn't matter if it was funny or not. The end result drew from comedy and drama, with some elements of fantasy and magical realism thrown in for good measure. There were no 'return to where you started' endings. We finished on cliffhangers, emotional beats, whatever felt right.

We managed to attract a very good cast. As well as Vic there was Alan Davies as Russell, Kate Ashfield as the girlfriend, the wonderful Josie Lawrence as her other lover Camilla, and Simone Bendix as the wife. That handsome rapscallion Patrick Robinson played Luis's love interest, Piers. The show was directed by comedy veteran Sandy Johnson and produced by Mia.

There was no studio audience and no canned laughter. A lot of the show was shot on location on a single camera, unlike a traditional sitcom, which used three-wall sets and four cameras. This would later become commonplace in the UK with great shows like *Outnumbered* and *Catastrophe*, but back in 2000 it was pretty radical and I was grateful that the BBC gave us the freedom to do it.

We spent a hefty chunk of our always-strained budget on music. Bryan Ferry sang the theme tune, and the soundtrack included artists such as Louis Prima, Al Green and Pink Martini.

I wouldn't say we got everything right. Sometimes we simply didn't have enough money to do an idea justice. And when it eventually went out on BBC2, some viewers were confused by the shifting tone. But overall I was thrilled with the result.

A Many Splintered Thing attracted a modest audience, but those who liked it really loved it. I was happy with that. The

American shows I revered, like *Taxi* and *Cheers*, all started small and built their following over time.

Reviews for the show were, unsurprisingly, much better than *Babes*. Some verged on the fawning. One described it as 'like classic Woody Allen, only set in Muswell Hill'. My wife had it mounted and framed and she hung it on the wall in my study. 'When you're depressed, just look at that,' she said. It was a lovely thing to do, but I have to tell you when she divorced me, I did as she advised and it didn't do fuck-all.

I was well into planning the next series when I received the news that *Splintered* had been axed. I was incredulous. How was that possible? Apparently there was a new controller at the BBC and, as ever, they were eager to make their mark with shows of their own. Mine didn't have a huge audience and wasn't yet established, so had been deemed dispensable to make way for the new. It was a terrible decision.

I'd now had one show with great viewing figures taken off because of lousy reviews and another that had been widely lauded cancelled because not enough people watched it.

The latter had hurt a lot more than the former. I'd given it my best shot and failed. My love affair with television was coming to an end.

We did make one more thing. *Back Home*, a World War II movie for ITV starring Sarah Lancashire adapted by Brian Finch from a book by Michelle Magorian. I did a little work on Brian's script but it wasn't a project I was heavily invested in. This was Mia's baby and a very good fist she made of it.

I learned three things working on *Back Home*. Sarah Lancashire was a brilliant actor and a dream to work with; I enjoyed the process of making a movie but was not by nature a producer. I had little interest in making something I hadn't written.

But as far as being a TV writer went, I was stuck. The

Splintered situation had more than taken the wind out of my sails. I didn't know what to do next. I had to find a way of moving forward.

That way was to close the company and write my first screenplay. I didn't consider the implications at any great length. It just felt like the right thing to do. If I had thought it through a little more thoroughly, I might have realised that back in those pre-streaming days, TV and film were two quite separate businesses. I was, in effect, starting over for the third time.

I'd never studied film writing or read any books on the subject or attended any courses. So I returned to the method that had served me well enough in music and TV. I immersed myself in what I considered the best examples of the genre, soaking it all up. I fancied writing a rom-com – probably a hangover from *Splintered* – so I watched *Annie Hall*, *When Harry Met Sally* and *Pretty Woman* on a loop for the next month or so.

I realised they had a lot in common with the better US sit-coms. Clearly defined characters, with the main story starting quickly and broken down into three acts. There was more to a movie, but I saw the same tricks and techniques cropping up frequently and noted them. What was welcome was that things moved forward and characters changed. They had to evolve to get what they wanted. In *Annie Hall*, Alvy's inability to change is the reason he doesn't end up with Annie, whom he adores. Harry (*When Harry Met Sally*) and Edward (*Pretty Woman*) become better men and so earn the right to live happily after.

My screenplay was called *The Perfect Margarita* and was loosely based on my life with a girl I'd once been involved with. Fortunately, my agent covered film as well as TV, so I showed it to her. She gave it the seal of approval and sent it out to pretty much anyone and everyone in the business. Over the next few months, I did the rounds and met them all. And everyone loved it. They raved about it. Couldn't say enough about how fabulous it was. I was a happy camper. My first film and it was going to get made. And it had been easy. Remember those last two sentences. They are absolute proof of what a *schmuck* I was, with zero notion of how the UK film business works.

When indeed it works at all.

I would learn over time that one of the reasons they all liked it so much was that it hadn't been through a development process. I'd just sat down and written it with no interference. The development process, for the uninitiated, is when a person or group of people who cannot write sit down with writers and tell them how and what they should be writing. Don't get me wrong, there are some wonderfully gifted individuals out there.

Producers, development executives and directors who can help make your script better. I've been lucky enough to work with a few. And they are rarer than unicorns that shit bricks of solid gold. Overwhelmingly, the development process is the morale-sapping disaster you might expect it to be.

I did not know any of this and sat back waiting for the offers from all those enthused producers to roll in. And I waited. And then I waited some more. Nothing. The happy camper became a miserable cunt. To quote the late Jackie Mason, 'I met a lot of producers. All most of them ever produced were business cards.'

Eventually, something did happen. Producers started inviting me in to talk about writing their projects.

Huh?

Here's how it breaks down. Getting a movie made is incredibly hard. People work their arses off for years to this end, and the vast majority fail. Their films never see the light of day. In such a tough and competitive environment, it's a widely held belief that projects with a provenance already in the public consciousness – a book adaptation, based on a hit video game, or even a novelty story that's been in the news – enjoy an inbuilt advantage. And you know what? They're probably right.

I think there's something else in play, though. Something less acknowledged.

Producers are only human. Well, some of them. And they like to feel that the project began with them.

It was their idea to option the rights to the book or whatever. It gives them a sense of authorship. Which is an enormous buzz to someone who cannot write. The dynamics of working with a writer who has created and written his own idea are entirely different and appeal less. It is possible to get your own project made, of course. It's just a harder slog.

Once they have their project, they need to employ a writer. Hence my flurry of recent invites. They genuinely liked my script and hoped I could do a similar job with theirs. That's wishful thinking for the most part. Your own thing was something you felt passionate about and believed in. Theirs would always be a paid gig. Then it would be subjected to the development process, with its potential to further degrade your best efforts.

Still, they were all opportunities for paid work as a screen-writer, which I was grateful to receive. I began to sift through them. My agent was very helpful. Not so much with assessing the projects as the producers who sent them. At any given time there's a tiny handful who stand a very good chance of getting a film made and a whole lot who never will. And, of course, all the rungs between them. These levels are not locked in. For one reason or another a company might have a window where they can get a film or two made. Then that window will close and they return to limbo. It's a tricky old business.

One producer's idea caught my eye but my agent nixed it immediately. 'Forget it. He's a two-bit crook.'

I bowed down to her experience on such matters. Several years later I got a call from her while she was in LA and she excitedly told me she'd run into this amazing producer and he wanted to have lunch with me. 'Great,' said I. 'who is it?' She told me the name.

'Hold up. Isn't he the two-bit crook?'

'Forget that. He's just had a huge hit with *******. He's red hot right now.'

There is no set profile for a film producer. Some are attracted by a genuine love of film. Many by the glamour. Others, often from a finance background, happen to be adept at raising money. Then there's an army of chancers, shysters and bottom-feeders.

One year at the Cannes Film Festival I found myself at a lavish party on an impressive-looking yacht moored in the old port. Champagne was flowing, and the great, the good and the gorgeous were having a ball. I didn't have a clue who or what the bash was in aid of. So I asked around. No one else seemed to know either. Finally, someone pointed out a bloke in his mid-thirties whom I didn't recognise. At a suitable point, I went over to say hi and thank him for his hospitality. But also to find out who the fuck he was.

I introduced myself and we got talking. He told me in a broad Scouse accent that he was a producer. You don't meet many movie producers from Liverpool, so well done him. He was clearly doing okay. As we chatted, something caught my attention. From a distance, he had looked suitably dressed for the occasion. Up close, his clothes looked cheap. More Matalan than Marc Jacobs. A few drinks in, the real story emerged. He had invested every penny he had in the yacht hire and a week of parties. That was his grand plan to break into the business. I wished him all the best and called it a night.

Another project I was sent was something entitled *Kinky Boots*. Apparently there'd been a short documentary on telly about a factory that was making women's shoes for men. Drag queens, transvestites, transexuals – or whatever the appropriate terminology is this week. It didn't sound much like a movie to me but the company had recently had a big hit with *Calendar Girls*. This meant their window to get another film made would be open wide. I took the meeting.

Calendar Girls was a film inspired by a real story about a bunch of Women's Institute ladies who stripped off for a nude calendar to raise money for leukaemia research after the husband of one of their members died from cancer. It had a lot in common with *The Full Monty*, an earlier film about a group of unemployed Northern steel workers who formed a striptease act to raise money, which had been enormously successful.

I met the production company and my takeaway from the meeting was that they saw *Kinky Boots* as being more of the same. I recall telling them I didn't like the title. Naming a film after an old Honor Blackman record? What folly!

I never bothered watching the docco, but drove to Northampton to meet the guy who was supposedly making the shoes. Without going into too much detail, I didn't come away entirely convinced by the whole shebang. This wasn't a huge issue. Most films inspired by real-life events detour significantly from what actually happened. That's why they're movies and not documentaries.

What was more of a problem was that I wasn't buying into a key element intrinsic to this type of story. Both *The Full Monty* and *Calendar Girls* were yarns about a group of people who overcame adversity by doing something mildly outrageous, i.e. getting their kit off. In *Kinky Boots* that risqué element would be the act of making women's shoes for men. Try as I may, I could not visualise a situation where eyebrows would raise and tongues would wag because a shoe manufacturer was making women's footwear in bigger sizes. What with it not being 1952 and all. I decided to pass.

Later that same night, I had a thought. What if the shoes were just a lead-in? An opportunity to introduce a character who would wear them. That would open up all kinds of interesting possibilities. And I happened to have just such a character tucked away in my back pocket. Luis/Tallulah from *A Many Splintered Thing*.

There were a host of reasons I'd enjoyed writing him so much. The conflicts within his/her twin persona and their shared basic humanity being top of the pile. I liked that the moral centre of the show was a gay man who dressed up as a woman.

It was also an opportunity to draw from my own history. Years spent hanging out at gay clubs and bars and various dodgy late-night watering holes. Especially those of a more exotic leaning. Chaguaramas in the seventies. The Piano Bar in the eighties. Once on leaving Chaguaramas I saw three glamorous-looking 'trannies' – as they then called themselves – frocks up and cocks out, pissing against a wall in Neal Street. 'Lovely out this time of night, innit?' said one loudly as I passed by.

Then there was my time touring the US gay circuit with Modern Romance. And of course, working with Divine after writing 'You Think You're a Man'. I'm a big John Waters fan, so had seen all the movies. But watching Divine on stage was something else. The words 'towering presence' fall short of doing him justice. And a huge contrast to when he was out of drag and always quietly spoken.

Bits of all this had informed Luis/Tallulah's character. Now, with *Kinky Boots*, there could be an opportunity to take it a step further. I began to feel excited.

I went back to the production company and pitched my idea. There's an art to pitching professionally and there are certain guidelines one can follow. I've never really bothered with all that. When I'm genuinely buzzing about something, I become hyper-enthused and animated. That's as close as I'm ever going to get to a pitching style. I'm self-aware enough to maybe crank it up a notch or two for the sake of theatre. But, essentially, what producers see and hear is my genuine passion for the project. The time they should worry is when I remain seated and talk calmly and coherently.

They seemed to respond positively. I suspected they were also talking to other writers and the few days' wait that followed was, shall we say, a trifle tense. Finally, I got the call. I would be writing *Kinky Boots*.

Any joy was short-lived, as we plunged straight into the development process. Which in this instance was thirty-something hours in one week, sitting in a room at the Bluebird Café in Chelsea talking to the three producers. Welcome to the Pleasuredome. It quickly became evident that they did not speak as one. Each had their own idea of what the film should be. At times I'd sit back, have another cup of coffee and watch as they argued it out amongst themselves. I heard the words *Calendar Girls* about 97 million times which, while understandable, was like dating a girl who kept banging on about her ex.

Eventually I forged a rough idea of what I could do to keep everyone – myself included – happy. I went away and wrote a treatment, which ran to about thirty pages. Treatments are a detailed blueprint of what you will be writing and are a required part of development. I don't much like writing them. Pages and pages of this happens and then that happens and then someone does this, are – without the benefit of dialogue – an incredibly boring read. And it's hard to excite producers with something that sends them to sleep.

Treatments also fly in the face of creativity. When I first write a character I know them pretty well. But I'm not a soothsayer. I cannot always accurately predict how they will respond in any given situation as things progress. They have the capacity to surprise. Which is, for me, the point where they come to life. What I put in a treatment is inspired guesswork at best. So getting too bogged down in specifics is a waste of energy. I like to work within the constraints of a rigid structure. But I need room to manoeuvre with what I choose to impress upon it. Technically speaking that's the 'being a writer' bit.

After they read the treatment there was another round of meetings. Again a lot of that time was producers 'debating' things amongst themselves. I knew a lot of what they were getting worked up about wouldn't amount to a hill of beans in the final movie. But I let them get on with it. I'd just zone out and plan what to have for dinner. Eventually I was given the go-ahead for a second draft of the treatment.

I went away and wrote another thirty-page document. There was some more discussion after that and finally, I was given the go-ahead to start the script. I was cream crackered before I'd even begun.

I worked hard and did a good job. I delivered it and again waited. What followed after is a blur. A seemingly endless cycle of meetings, notes and rewrites that went on until I was punch-drunk. The more refined the story was getting the more challenging the three-producer thing became. And the spectre of *Calendar Girls* always loomed large. It's a perfectly inoffensive movie, but I was starting to fucking hate it.

I was making progress, though. They liked all the key elements. Old Mr Price dying suddenly and leaving the family shoe factory to his immature son Charlie, who had zero interest in following in the old man's footsteps. Him discovering that the business was on the verge of bankruptcy and trying to save it for the sake of the employees, who he had come to like and respect. His growing feelings for Lauren, a working-class girl at the factory who's as smart as a whip and gives him the idea about making shoes for niche markets. His posh fiancée, who wants him to sell up so they can start a new life in London. And of course the chance meeting with Tallulah – as she was then still called – which sets him on the road to salvation and fetish footwear, climaxing with a catwalk procession of drag-queen models. All of this worked really well.

There was a problem, though. A big one.

The producers had a deal with Miramax. Relax – Harvey didn't try and get me into the shower to give him a handie. Never met the geezer. Miramax was owned by Disney, and while they were never physically present at script meetings, it became clear to me they were terrified of Tallulah. Pulling her back was the only thing the three producers always agreed on.

When not performing, the Tallulah I had written went home to a quiet life alone as Simon. A gay man who'd been hurt in the past and had lost friends to AIDS. As a result, he now shied away from relationships. His world appeared glamorous but was actually rather sad.

Nothing was seen of this past life; it was simply information to be picked up as we went along, which would mark the character as a living, breathing entity. It also perfectly set him up as not quite functioning properly. Something his adventures in shoe business would help repair, and facilitate finding true love at the end of the movie. It's a story of two men emerging from shadows. Charlie from his dad's, Simon from his past. Poignant and rather fucking charming, if I say so myself.

And they would have none of it. Not a motherfucking beat. AIDS? Past relationships? A love story with another man? Not a chance. It was even pointed out to me that 'drag queens don't have to be gay, you know'. I guess they had a point. It is possible to have a straight drag queen. Just as it's possible to have a transexual Chancellor of the Exchequer. Personally speaking, though, I have never run into either.

Talullah had been the key to my getting involved in *Kinky Boots*. I now felt like they wanted to reduce her to a bloke who wore a dress. When the film finally came out, 'Lola' – as she had by then been renamed, no doubt after the old Kinks' tune – did not even feature on the posters. The actor, Chiwetel Ejiofor, was pictured as alter ego Simon, looking dapper in a three-piece whistle, shirt and tie.

The first press release I saw described Lola as a 'cabaret artist'. They even swerved the words 'drag queen'. I'd presented them with a complex and colourful breakout character and they were embarrassed by her.

I'd put in a long, hard shift and was tired, drained and more than a little dispirited. It's conceivable that I was also a little 'oversensitive'. That happens. But I'd come to the end of the road. I cannot recall if I jumped, was pushed or it was by mutual consent. But I was done with *Kinky Boots*.

The producers hired Tim Firth to take over. No surprise there. Tim had taken over from the original writer, Juliette Towhidi on – you got it – *Calendar Girls*, and had even been given pole position in the writing credits.

I met Juliette, an immensely likeable and intelligent Iranian woman, years later and we became mates. On a couple of occasions, we compared war wounds. She had been battered about by the process and still bore the bruises.

I was more fortunate. I take everything on the chin while it's happening. The minute it's over, I have a disturbing capacity to place things in a box, neatly tie it with a ribbon, and bury it away deep for ever more. It's the least Jewy, most English thing about me.

Not quite so easy on *Kinky Boots*, mind you.

The producers gave me first writing credit, which I had expected but appreciated. I went along to the premiere but left half an hour into the movie. It had nothing to with anything I saw on screen. The director, Julian Jarrold, appeared to have done a sterling job and the cast was uniformly excellent. And I loved the opening scene – which I had not written – of a young Simon dancing around in girl's shoes to Bowie's 'Prettiest Star'. It was more my own residual disappointment.

I eventually watched the film properly when it was shown on telly. With the passage of time, I enjoyed it. Some names, locations and details had changed and Tim had naturally put some things into his own words. But it was still the story and characters I had created. I recall only one scene making me bang my head against the wall repeatedly. Lola beating Don, the factory bigot, in an arm-wrestling contest in front of all his workmates. For a story that looked at different aspects of what it was to be a man, I felt victory via physical strength sent out the exact wrong message. In my version, it had been a verbal takedown. But I guess that all comes back to how you see the character and the movie.

The producers got the *Kinky Boots* they wanted. It did okay at the box office but never came close to emulating the success of *Calendar Girls*.

After all that, I was immersed in new films and moved on. But *Kinky Boots* refused to go away entirely.

Daryl Roth, a Tony Award-winning producer and Hal Luftig, a Tony and Olivier Award-winning producer, had both seen the film independently and thought it perfect source material for a Broadway musical. They teamed up and in 2007 secured the stage rights.

I'd already said to my agent that I thought it would have been better suited to the stage, so this was interesting news. Which only got better when Harvey Fierstein was later drafted in to write the book. I'd seen his *Torch Song Trilogy* and loved it. In fact, it was probably remiss of me not to list it along with my other influences when first writing Tallulah/Lola. He had also written the book to *La Cage aux Folles*. Harvey was the perfect shout.

He and Cyndi Lauper were good friends, which opened the door to her coming on board to write the songs. Again not too shabby.

I had nothing to do with the making of the musical. There was a little contact with Harvey and we discussed a few minor things he wasn't clear on. He was psyched about the project and promised he'd give it his best shot. Of that, I had no doubt. I also received a delightful note from La Lauper thanking me for 'the wonderful source material'. I had not met her and was taken by her good grace. Girl's a class act.

Kinky Boots, starring Billy Porter as Lola – the ultimate in dream casting – eventually opened on Broadway in 2013. The rest, as they say at the Academy of Forbidden Clichés, is history. It ran forever and was a smash hit in both the US and the West End. Ultimately it played in six countries on four continents, from Seoul to Sydney, collecting a stack of bling along the way. That first year it earned thirteen nominations and six Tony wins, including Best Musical, Best Actor for Billy Porter and Best Score. The cast album also picked up a

Grammy. In the UK the show won a Laurence Olivier Award for Best New Musical.

It found its way into the public consciousness, which made me smile. Not sure if it was pride or amusement or a mixture of both. Back in the Modern Romance days I'd once seen a thousand or so kids on a beach in Ibiza dance in a conga line to our first hit 'Everybody Salsa'. I sat back and watched, sipping on my beer and thought to myself, *I did that.* Seeing *Kinky Boots* mentioned on *Friends* and then *Gilmore Girls* gave me a similar buzz. It had been through a few evolutions along the way, but knowing that a fair bit of what had started life in my nut had come so far was definitely better than a slap around the boat with a wet kipper.

I went to the opening night in London and also some subsequent productions. I enjoyed them all. Harvey had delivered on his promise. I had never mentioned the things I felt were missing from the script to him, so knew they would not be in the show. I was pleased to see that it was still very recognisable as the story and characters I had written. Some of my lines and a few gags were still fully intact. It being a musical, Lola was finally presented with the kind of gusto she had always merited. The entire show had. It was a triumph. Harvey had very deftly pushed the comparable journeys of Charlie and Lola to the fore. He had framed it a little differently, making it just about both characters' relationships with their fathers. And it worked perfectly.

Without the other elements I always felt would be necessary, please note. We live and we learn.

My son Otis entered the room while I was writing this and as is often my way I got him to take a look over what I'd done so far and to give me his thoughts. This led to us talking about the show and that part of my life. He asked how I felt about it all.

I told him it was complicated. I was thrilled to have played my part in something that had gone so far. But well, you know. There were caveats.

'It's difficult to sum up an experience like that in a few words.'

He looked at me with a deadpan expression. 'Bittersweet,' he said before walking away.

Smart little fuck.

HORSE RIDING
IN MONGOLIA

Sitting in a bar called the Cathouse in Eureka Springs (population 2,000) in Arkansas, enjoying a beer and Wild Turkey breakfast with my buddy, Stiff-Neck Steve. I should point out that Steve is not usually known by this handle. He's just plain Steve. But he has a stiff neck resulting in his head being angled at a constant tilt. The pain and restricted movement are a constant annoyance, but he's more concerned about optics.

'People are going to call me Stiff-Neck Steve,' he says.

'Don't be ridiculous,' I reply.

The thirty-hour day of travelling we were recovering from had been terminally unpleasant. The only bright spot being when I was caught in the X-ray check at Atlanta Airport and the young black dude from Customs and Excise announced loudly that I had a 'groin anomaly' showing up on the screen.

'What is that?' he asked.

'My penis?' I suggested helpfully.

This did not bring forth the appreciative peals of laughter I had craved, and he called over two colleagues. The phrase 'groin anomaly' was then bandied about like a shuttlecock between them. Finally, he told me he would have to pat my groin down and asked me if I would prefer this to be done in private. 'No mate,' I replied. 'Knock yourself out.' He gave me a very public squeeze around the crown jewels and his hand eventually settled on my Zippo lighter in the deep recesses of the pocket of my Nigel Cabourn overalls.

I realised what it was immediately, not having had an erection that hard since 1986.

We eventually caught a connecting flight to our destination, Fayetteville, and emerged ten hours behind schedule at 1.30 a.m. The one bit of luck we had that day was the area's sole Uber driver turned up within three minutes of me booking him and in just over another hour had dropped us off at our hotel. Which was, of course, closed and locked up for the night. We were in the Ozarks and it was bitterly cold. Our brains had long since ceased functioning so it didn't occur to us to phone. Instead, we banged on the door repeatedly, loud enough to wake the dead. The manager, who as it turns out wasn't dead at all, greeted us with a smile and warmly welcomed us in. God bless America. He led us to our suite and I was asleep in no time at all.

Despite the previous day's exertions, I awoke early and went out for a walk. Eureka Springs is a speck of a town built onto the side of the Ozark Mountains, which I had expected, but also something of a tourist spot, which I had not. It was off-season and the few shops open specialised in tut and were much the same as tut emporiums the world over. No toothpaste or moisturiser, which I needed, but plenty of mugs with 'I went to the Eureka Springs and bought this cunty mug' written on them, and suchlike. On my way back to the hotel, the somewhat optimistically named Grand Central, I bumped into Steve, who was also out taking a constitutional, and he dragged me into the bar. It had just gone 10 a.m. and we sat drinking and chatting with our bar lady, Jinette, who looked and sounded like she'd wandered in off the set of peak period *Roseanne*. Back when its star was crazy enough to marry Tom Arnold but not yet support Donald Trump.

About an hour in, a man named Jay entered and talked privately to Jinette. She then returned to work, dabbing at her eyes with a tissue. 'Is everything okay?' I asked. 'My husband just passed,' she said. They'd been married sixteen years and separated for the last four. 'But he was still my friend,' she added, as if to explain away her tears. Like any explanation was necessary. He'd been taken poorly a few days ago and admitted to hospital. And that, as it turned out, had been that.

Death is always a shock. Even when it's expected and, on occasions, a long time coming. But this really had come out of left field. We extended our condolences and I told her she should go home. 'This is my job,' she said. 'I can't just leave.' Working-class people, man. Not for nothing a country's backbone.

Barkeeps the world over are adept at tapping into your life and saying just enough to keep you talking. With roles reversed, we struggled to find the right things to say. It felt wrong being there at such a private moment. We drank up, paid up, and left. Overtipping almost enough to cover the funeral expenses. Back at the hotel, I crashed out for the rest of the day.

I was eventually awoken by the phone and Stiff-Neck telling me, 'I'm at the Basin Park Hotel. Get over here.' Ever compliant, I did as instructed.

The hotel was the venue for the Ozark Mountain Music Festival, an annual American roots music event, and the reason we were in town. More specifically in my case, to see Willy Tea Taylor, a guitar-picking cattleman's son, with a voice that breaks your heart and a way with words that can

257

put it back together again. I've been listening to his music for years and have always wanted to see him perform in his natural habitat. This seemed as good a time as any.

The hotel was busy and full of men with beards and denim overalls. It was like Shoreditch High Street on a Saturday. I found Stiff-Neck in the games room talking to an attractive blonde woman in her late forties. Her name was Jonette. All we needed now was a Junette, Janette and Jenette and we'd have the full set. She was from Illinois and sold hardwood flooring for a living. Jonette was open and friendly, as was everyone we met in Eureka Springs. She spoke a lot about her son. 'He was a very successful lawyer and he just quit. Now he has dreadlocks and keeps alpacas. What you gonna do?' she asked no one in particular.

Have him put down, I thought, but kept it to myself.

After that, we got sucked into a happy vortex of pickled jalapeño margaritas, great music and new friends for life. Or the next few days, at the very least. My favourite of these was Mike and Squeak, a young couple from Baylis, Illinois, a town which, at the last count, boasted just 200 residents. 'We're not actually from Baylis,' explained Mike, 'but that's the biggest town close by.' 'Just cows and corn, man,' chipped in his other half, 'that's all there is.' They were both born of poor farming stock and Squeak had her son when she was fifteen. Despite the misleading moniker – a childhood nickname that stuck around – she was a real firecracker of a young woman. Petite, talkative and highly animated. She and her boyfriend had driven for seven hours to be there, and had no money. I asked how they were going to manage. She threw me a prizewinning smile. 'I'm pretty and Mike's a real smooth talker. We get by.'

Her ever-present water flask full of Fireball whiskey and soda no doubt helped a little too. Mike explained where they came from, whiskey was a way of life. 'Tractor don't go? You drink whiskey. You get sick and got no healthcare? You drink whiskey.'

The musical highlight that first night was the Eureka Strings. I'm not sure how many of them were on stage in the main ballroom. Ukes, guitars, keys, fiddles, a dungaree-wearing double-bass player, and a very large woman blowing the daylights out of a clarinet. Vocals were shared by a couple dressed in classic Country & Western cowboy and cowgirl regalia.

The band's sound bounced around like a pinball, rico-cheting off bluegrass, country, blues and Appalachian folk. At one stage the glorious cacophony they were whipping up was so close to soul music, you could spit at it. They threw in a few covers. The Dixie funk of 'Midnight in Harlem' and a rousing rendition of Jimmie Rodgers' ol' time country tune 'In the Jailhouse Now'. I celebrated the latter by dancing around like George Clooney in *O Brother, Where Art Thou?* One happy Jew rose amongst the thorns.

The next day we were strolling around, taking in nothing much of interest, when a tram slowed down and the driver, Larry, asked if we needed a ride. He was heading up Magnetic Mountain to Christ of the Ozarks, a much-mentioned local landmark. Both in need of some redemption, we jumped on board and ten minutes later alighted at a sixty-five-foot white statue of Jesus, arms outstretched towards the town below. I suspect he's meant to be gathering in his flock. But his arms were too straight and it looked more like he was playing air-planes. Or that someone had half-inched his cross. Either way, I didn't feel much inclined to be welcomed into his bosom. The monument had been commissioned by Gerald L. K. Smith, a clergyman, politician and far-right demagogue. Not to mention racist, virulent anti-Semite, Holocaust denier and

Nazi sympathiser. I bet he was a hoot at dinner parties. That his lasting legacy looked like it had been whittled from an enormous bar of soap by the village tard was most pleasing.

I never heard anything to suggest the local people held similarly unsavoury views. And Stiff-Neck's standard gambit when we entered a bar or diner, 'Excuse me, would you mind serving two elderly homosexuals?' was largely ignored. Perhaps because while addressing the owner, he was usually looking at the door.

Eureka Springs didn't strike me as your standard hillbilly haven. For one thing, a lot of old hippies seem to have washed up there. It was more the kind of town where they called crafts 'art'. We also heard a lot of talk of ghosts and spirits and hauntings, which folk appeared to take seriously. When I looked at the paintings being created by local artists in the festival's merch-room-cum-activity area, I too became open to the notion of a malign presence at work. Maybe it was also responsible for me just using the word 'folk'.

That second day at the festival was altogether more staid. Though the hail of 'hi Steves' and 'hey Geoffs' from people neither of us remembered bore testimony to the fun had the previous night. I was wearing my blanket-lined Carhartt jacket again, as it was the only warm coat I had with me. At some point, I put my hand in my side pocket and pulled out a bag of weed. Now I don't smoke weed and have certainly never bought any. Not a clue how it got there. I contributed it to the Mike and Squeak subsistence fund and it was received with thanks.

At around midnight, we headed over to Chelsea's, a late-night café and dive bar popular amongst musicians. I fell into convo with a girl named Danielle who told me she'd once been dropped naked in Equatorial Africa with only a machete and left to survive for three weeks. My immediate reaction was that she was a mental. But it was worse. She had been a reality-show contestant on the Discovery Channel. She'd survived the ordeal but had lost forty-five pounds in the process – she didn't look like her fighting weight was much over 130 now – and was still feeling the physical side effects three years on. She used the phrase 'butt- meat deterioration' a lot, which I had trouble surviving, so I excused myself and headed for the crowded bar.

When I decided to come and see Willy Tea Taylor play at the festival – about a week and a half earlier – it had occurred to me that at such a small event I might have the opportunity to meet him. Initially I warmed to the prospect, but after turning things over in my head, I decided that wasn't such a good idea. Meeting people you admire is an unbalancing act. It can be awkward and disappointing. I was there for the man's music, not to shake his hand. It was best left at that.

The dude in front of me picked up his beers off the counter and as he turned, he offered a broad smile and a friendly 'hey, man'. The long red beard which made my own facial growth look like a five o'clock shadow was unmistakable. 'My name's Willy,' he said.

'I know,' I replied. I told him we were there to see him play.

'That's cool, brother. Where you from?'

'London.'

'You serious?'

'I am.'

'What's your name?'

'Geoff.'

'Good to make your acquaintance, Geoff. I think you and I need to have a drink.'

Willy called over his buddy Jared, and I took them over to meet Stiff-Neck. They had driven from Willy's home in Nashville for the following day's show and after that would be heading off to Tulsa for the next. Which, when not writing or recording, was pretty much how they lived their lives.

I asked how he managed, spending so much time on the road. 'We listen to music and a lot of audiobooks,' Willy told us. And we were off. Over the surrounding bar room hubbub, the four of us got down to exchanging notes on what we like to read and listen to. They were two extremely bright guys, as keen to hear about our passions as they were to share their own. Steve, who has been obsessed with all things Americana since I first met him over thirty years ago, was in his element. Watching him and Willy debate the merits of Sam Shepard – Willy pro/Steve less convinced – was a blast. The conversation remained lively and entertaining well into the early hours, pausing only for further refreshment. Woodie Guthrie, John Steinbeck, William Faulkner, John Prine, Jack Kerouac . . . iconic names were kicked around like they were old drinking buddies. When I felt out of my depth – which was not infrequent – I shut up and listened. There was a lot worth listening to that night. But eventually the margaritas and jet lag came to collect. When Danielle joined us and promptly reintroduced the matter of her 'butt-meat deterioration' it was my cue to say *buenas noches*.

Willy's show the next day was close to perfect. I say close because two boozed-up rednecks at the back insisted on talking loudly through the first half dozen tunes. From the wilds of Kentish Town to the Ozarks, it seems to me people have forgotten how to behave at gigs. Drives me nuts, and I felt myself tensing up. I did my breathing exercises to restore calm.

Breathe in red.

CUNTS.

Breathe out pink.

IGNORE THE CUNTS.

Eventually the music won them over and they quietened down. Or maybe they'd just used up all the words they knew. Who can say? Willy lightened the mood in the room with a version of John Prine and Iris DeMent's 'In Spite of Ourselves', singing both the male and female verses. From there on it was one classic self-penned tune after another, many of which I'd heard hundreds of times before but only ever in my own home. This was altogether different. When he picked out the intro to the plaintive 'Big Jim's Guitar' – a song about his late grandparents that always gets to me – I began to feel overwhelmed. It was the man, the song, the words, *that voice,* and of course the where. But it was more than that. It was me, my time of life, my hopes and fears, my dreams and disappointments. And a lot of other things that felt very personal to me but are common to all of us. Great art can do that to a man and the tears began to fall.

'See,' whispered Stiff-Neck, 'you are a homosexual.'

That night the four of us had dinner together. There were a lot of laughs and a lot more talk about stuff we liked. The convo was less literature and more music-based, so I felt on firmer ground. Though Willy and I discovered a shared love of Jim Harrison, and I was happy to recommend *The Raw and the Cooked: Adventures of a Roving Gourmand* as a book you cannot read too many times. I've bought it three times and still don't have a copy on my bookshelves. Borrow as much as you like, kids, but never a lender be.

It turned out that Willy and Jared were both movie buffs and had seen *Kinky Boots* and were fans. It also turned out that Stiff-Neck Steve, my friend of over thirty years standing, had never bothered to watch it. 'I've been busy,' he explained, and laughter spread around the table once again.

Willy asked me if I ever used pencils to write. I said that I didn't, but usually carried a Field Notes book and pencil to jot down any ideas I had. He produced two new pencils and handed them to me. Palomino Blackwing 42s. 'Try these,' he said. 'I write everything with them.' I thanked him and slipped them inside my jacket pocket.

The evening reached a head with Willy pitching us to all go horse riding in Mongolia the following year. Everyone agreed that was a sterling idea and a lot of enthused chatter followed. It would be great to meet up again. And it's important to keep doing new things.

As we paid the bill and stood up to leave, it took my lower vertebrae thirty seconds longer than the rest of my body to straighten out. I may even have made the 'old guy getting up' noise. I pulled out one of my new pencils and made a quick note to get that looked at before Mongolia.

NB. The Palomino Blackwing 42 pencil is a tribute to Jackie Robinson. On 6 July 1944, eleven years before Rosa Parks refused to move to the back of the bus in Montgomery, Alabama and ignited the civil rights movement, Second Lieutenant Jack Roosevelt Robinson, as he was then known, did the same thing. His refusal earned him a court-martial for 'behaving with disrespect' and 'willful disobedience of lawful command'. Lieutenant Robinson stood his ground at trial and was acquitted of all charges. After being honourably discharged, he signed a contract with the Kansas City Monarchs baseball club. A few years later, Jack 'Jackie' Robinson was called up to play Major Leagues Baseball by the Brooklyn Dodgers, breaking the colour barrier and providing much-needed momentum to the desegregation movement, which extended well beyond baseball.